ACCEPTING YOUR BLENDED FAMILY

Edited by: Frances Sharpe
                    francessharpe.com

Book Design by: Aaron Davis
                    aarondavis.net

Cover Artwork by: Rebecca Baruc
                    beccabaruc.com

Any people depicted in images have given approval by their estate and trustees. This book is printed on acid-free paper.

Because of the dynamic nature of the Internet, any web addresses or links contained in this book may have changed since publication and may no longer be valid.

ACCEPTING YOUR BLENDED FAMILY

A Handbook for Life After Divorce

by Wendy Smith Baruc

Kingsbury Road Creative

To Ian and Olivia, my children,

And Shirley, my mother

Because you are the reason I am who I am.

You are the reason for my desire to grow and change.

You are the sweetest part of me, and I love you

more than tongue can tell.

— TABLE OF CONTENTS —

Introduction

Chapter One
When a Relationship Leads to Divorce...1

Chapter Two
Trade In Your "Me-Centric" Attitude for the Sake of the Children.............21

Chapter Three
The Problem with Playing the Blame Game..49

Chapter Four
Dating Post-Divorce and Introducing New Partners...............................69

Chapter Five
Integrating First and Second Families After Remarriage.........................95

Chapter Six
Ongoing Life as a Blended Family...117

Chapter Seven
Dealing with Difficult People in the Blended Family..............................151

Chapter Eight
The Seven Most Harmful Social Taboos for Blended Families....................173

Chapter Nine
Lessons from Families Working Together
and Becoming Healthier Tribes...189

Acknowledgments

About the Author

INTRODUCTION

In 2010, I took my 21-year-old son and 18-year-old daughter to the Yasawa Islands in Fiji for a holiday—just the three of us. I had wanted to take them on a holiday like this for a long time, but because of my financial situation at the time, it didn't seem possible. But then we were on our way, and I was so grateful.

That vacation might not have happened if it weren't for the support of one woman. My former husband's wife, now my children's stepmother as well as the mother of my children's two half brothers. We had grown closer out of cooperation and the need to work together so life would flow more easily for the ones we both loved. Over time, we grew to be friends and then became family. We joined together. We blended.

When my former husband and I met and fell in love, both our families were very happy for us. For a long time, our marriage and life together provided a grounding force and a safe haven. Our union also signaled that all had turned out well for our families. We shared a lot of good times and happiness together. We had two beautiful children, and that has always been a source of great joy for both of us.

We had both experienced some damage during our childhoods, but we managed to keep all that at bay for the most part until after our children were born. That's when the issues seemed to really show themselves and began to surface, and we both started to experience some trauma. At the time, I was unaware how much childhood damage could impact our adult lives. Unfortunately, communication became very difficult, and we simply did not have the tools to deal with what came up for us.

We separated. Hearts were broken, and the world in which we all had lived so peacefully began to fall apart. At first, I had very little understanding about what was actually happening to me or why my marriage was falling apart. There didn't seem to be anything I could do about it except struggle. I felt judged. I felt wronged. We tried to seek help. We went to therapy. We attended self-help seminars. We made new friends. We changed our lives. But mostly, we hurt, hurt, hurt.

Eventually, we divorced. It felt like I was jumping off a cliff and taking my children with me. I was bad now. I was the bad one. I was to blame. I was the problem. I felt ashamed. I tried to justify my position. In the beginning, there was so much hurt between us, but lashing out at each other didn't feel right.

At the same time, my sibling was also getting divorced, which meant my mother was going through the breakup of both her children's marriages. This was very tough on her. My mother had raised us by herself with no help from my father. None! At that time, a single woman raising children on her own was practically unheard of. When my mother finally saw both her children marry lovely people and have beautiful children of their own, she felt joy that things had turned out well. But with two divorces pending, it was all coming apart, and we were all so sad and angry. And the children were in the middle of all this strife. My mother had always been my rock, but now she too was slipping off the cliff, and we were all struggling.

Somehow, I managed to pull myself together and started thinking about my children. I once heard a woman, who was talking about her very young children after her divorce, say, "If I'm okay, then my children will be okay. If my needs are met, then I can take care of them." I think she got it backwards. In my view, "If my children are okay, then I'll be okay. If my children's needs can be met, then I can take care of myself."

This became my motto. I had young children at home and they were at the mercy of me and my decisions. I made a lot of mistakes at first as I began my search for better role models and a better way to do this.

We shifted our focus, and although divorced, we realized we were going to have to figure out how to be a family and how to develop a new family structure going forward. My former husband and my mother had shared a very close relationship. He had become like another son to her, and they really loved each other. He was a very important member of the family, and he had helped to make our family stronger and more connected. He was so loved and valued by everyone in our family. And, we all knew that the children still loved both of us, and they were looking for stability and reassurance.

We wanted to keep our family together as much as possible. So we did our best to be together as a family with the children on holidays and at school functions. We helped each other with problems.

We did it for the sake of the children.

We did it for the sake of the whole family.

I did it for myself too.

We weren't married anymore, but we still could have the family we built around us, and I needed that more than ever.

I remember thinking very clearly at some point that when people divorce they leave each other, not the family. But that wasn't the message I was getting from my divorced friends or in the media. According to them, divorce was supposed to be like a war zone. I didn't want to live like that, and I didn't want to subject my children to that either, so I began creating my own set of new rules to live by. My former husband and his new wife, as well as my mother were all on board too. Open-hearted and open-minded, they were all willing to work together with me to make up our own minds about our family life. It was the silver lining to a very dark cloud.

We had to be pioneers because we weren't seeing any examples of healthy post-divorce behavior around us. We really had to create a relationship based on our own sense of what was going to make our family thrive. One of the things I learned along the way was that, wherever you go, there you are. I had to keep turning inward for direction on how to act, what to say, and how to go on from where I was. This self-reflection proved invaluable in the process.

When the going got tough, we were able to help each other. Maybe it was out of necessity at first, but it soon became normal for us as we became a blended family. Instead of waging war, we created more love and provided resources for each other and for all our children. People would approach us when they saw the two of us working together, laughing, and enjoying each other's company. They wanted to know how we did it, how the former wife and the new wife could get along so well.

Occasionally, I would encounter someone who expressed discomfort or even anger with our choices, but I told myself they were just holding on to old patterns. I did my best to rise above the criticism.

Now, years later, we have never spent a holiday or important event apart from our children. As long as they were young and living at home with us, we chose to include all of us. We didn't trade off years or make the children choose where to go or whom to invite for a special occasion. "We gather," as my mother puts it. We are a family. We are a blended family. We are a tribe.

People around us saw how we were accepting family, and they started asking me for help to navigate their own divorce situations. As my practice as a relationship counselor grew, I began working with families going through separations and remarriage. Many of them suggested I write about it. "You should write a book," they said. And so I began writing down their stories—some sad, some inspiring—and started documenting the strategies I was using with them to develop healthier ways to work through divorce, remarriage, and blending families. This book is the result of that work. It is the book I wish I had when I was going through my own divorce. Actually, it is the book I wish I had read before I even got married. I hope you find it useful in your journey.

THE CONSEQUENCES OF DIVORCE AND REMARRIAGE

I am not the only one with a blended family. About 42 million adults in the United States have been married more than once, nearly twice as many as in 1980, according to Pew Research Center. As second and third marriages become more common, the number of children affected by those unions also rises. According to the National Center for Health Statistics, over 60 percent of remarried women are in blended families with children. I call the new family structure a blended family, a tribe, and, unfortunately, many of them are fraught with dysfunction.

That's because the pain of divorce, which some liken to the trauma of war, can carry over into your expanded family. Any unresolved issues from a first marriage can cast an even wider web, spreading beyond that nuclear family to ensnare new spouses, stepchildren, in-laws, and even friends. The results can be explosive, leading to destructive behaviors and even more heartbreak. 40 to 50 percent of first marriages end in divorce. This is bad enough but then on top of that, 67 percent of second marriages and 74 percent of third marriages ultimately dissolve ending in divorce as well.

In the face of these dire statistics, it is shocking that as a society we haven't focused on divorce as a social epidemic, the way we've committed to finding solutions for other issues such as mental health, homelessness, and bullying. The consequences of divorce are creating more and more emotionally damaged people in our society, and we all end up paying the price for this. We live in a world of increasingly fractured families. As a result, our social fabric is fraying at a breakneck pace.

SOCIAL TABOOS AND MYTHS SURROUNDING DIVORCE

In part, this is due to a host of social taboos and myths surrounding divorce that reinforce its damaging effects. The social norms that dictate how we treat and engage former partners, new boyfriends/girlfriends, and stepchildren are often destructive. Just look at this sampling of long-held myths and social taboos:

- Former husbands and wives can never be at the same event so family and friends have to choose to disinvite one of them.

- Divorced couples must maintain separate lives and train their children, family, friends, and even their children's teachers to respect and enforce these new boundaries.

- It is normal for one former spouse to assign blame in order to villainize, ostracize, or exclude the other partner.

- It is socially acceptable for former partners to speak poorly or negatively about their former partner in front of their children.

- Children are expected to adapt to the most uncomfortable situations while the parents avoid awkward settings.

Considering how destructive these behaviors are for our children and families as well as our friends and communities, why do we continue to cling to them? The time to change is now.

CREATING A LOVING BLENDED FAMILY

In this book, I will shatter these myths and introduce you to better ways to navigate divorce and remarriage so you can have a healthier, happier, more loving family. As a relationship counselor, I have helped hundreds of couples and families negotiate the difficult issues and bumps in the road that come with divorce and blended families. I teach them new behaviors and more effective ways to communicate so they can create a more functional tribe.

One of the first things I do with my clients is encourage them to use the term "former partner" rather than "ex." You'll find that I use this term throughout this book. Words are so important, and the word "ex" carries a negative, adversarial connotation. "Former partner" or "former husband/wife" sounds much more cooperative and helps get you in the mindset that the two of you are in this together. I also like the fact that former partner is more inclusive and can apply whether you were legally married or in a long-term relationship, and whether it was a same-sex or opposite-sex relationship.

As a body-mind-spirit coach for three decades, I also encourage my clients to be more open and self-reflective, and I guide them to make profound changes in their lives. You and your family can make these powerful shifts too. This book will provide you with the transformational tools and proven strategies to do it.

HOW TO USE THIS BOOK

This book is intended to be a handbook that you can refer to often. Feel free to skip around to the chapters that are most relevant to you now and then go back to the others. This book can provide guidance whether you are in the midst of a divorce or already in a blended family in your second or third marriage.

Within each chapter, you'll explore many aspects of divorce, re-marriage, and blending families in order to help you create a stronger tribe. You'll find helpful "DOs & DON'Ts" that show you how to flip the switch on detrimental thinking patterns and negative communication styles. In addition, a "Next Steps" section at the end of each chapter is included to help you make practical changes based on the advice in this book. Also included is a "Chapter Highlights" section that will emphasize the main points to remember.

Note that some concepts are repeated throughout the chapters. This is intentional because these ideas are foundational to the success of any family and bear repeating.

Here's a preview of what you'll learn in each chapter.

- **Chapter 1** introduces strategies to help you navigate divorce and find ways to communicate in a positive and healthy manner as your relationship changes.

- **Chapter 2** reveals why it is essential to put your children and their needs first in every situation and shows how to overcome unrealistic expectations when it comes to children dealing with divorce.

- **Chapter 3** explores how blaming your former partner for the failure of your marriage or harboring resentment and hatred toward them can put your tribe in jeopardy and offers tips to help you reframe your thinking and gain a healthier perspective.

- **Chapter 4** takes a closer look at the challenges of dating after divorce when you have children and provides guidelines to help you introduce a new partner to your family.

- **Chapter 5** examines the pitfalls that come from integrating first and second families and offers strategies to overcome them so you can create a healthier blended family.

- **Chapter 6** details the drama that can come with ongoing life as a blended family and provides suggestions for parenting and stepparenting, ways to help children cope with new siblings, tips to help you survive the holidays, and more.

- **Chapter 7** takes a look at the difficult people who disrupt family dynamics and delivers a set of tools you and your tribe can use to handle even the most toxic personalities.

- **Chapter 8** offers an overview of the seven most harmful social taboos and myths that can challenge your progress and shows you how to prevent them from negatively impacting your tribe.

- **Chapter 9** introduces you to blended families who are doing it right and shows you what you can learn from them so you can strengthen your own tribe.

HAPPIER FAMILIES, HEALTHIER SOCIETY

Accepting family is the greatest thing you can do for yourself, your children, and your blended family. But that's not all. If more people dedicated the time and attention to incorporating the teachings in this book into their daily lives, we could create a more loving society. Maybe we can't make ourselves or others stay married, but we can learn to cope with divorce and remarriage in a smarter, more compassionate way.

With the tools described in this book, our society can aim to transform the social epidemic of divorce into an opportunity to strengthen extended families and community ties. Perhaps as we build better relationships at home, we can in turn construct a healthier society that is more open, interdependent, and resilient. And that is something that can benefit everyone for generations to come.

CHAPTER ONE

WHEN A RELATIONSHIP LEADS TO DIVORCE

"Chains do not hold a marriage together. It is threads, hundreds of tiny threads, which sew people together through the years."

— Simone Signoret

When we say "I do" we believe, or at least we hope, it will be forever. And for much of American history, this was true for the vast majority of couples. In the 1950s, less than 20 percent of marriages ended in divorce. In those days, you had to prove infidelity or cruelty to dissolve a marriage. Fast-forward to the 1970s after no-fault divorces were introduced, and the rates skyrocketed. By 1980, 52 percent of marriages ended in divorce. Rather than viewing divorce as a desperate measure, couples began divorcing due to "irreconcilable differences." Today, 40 to 50 percent of all marriages end in divorce, and it is often based on feelings surrounding love, connection, and personal happiness, not just as a last resort. Though marriage and divorce have gone through some external changes over time, internal changes in our perceptions and standards are needed if we are going to build and sustain a healthier generation of children who are growing up in divorced families.

ENTERING MARRIAGE WITH BLINDERS ON

Marriage is such an important step in our lives, but many of us enter into it without a plan or any serious preparation. We're caught up in the romance of it all and the notion of happily ever after. We put more diligent effort into other more mundane things, like getting a driver's license. To earn your driver's license, you have to study a handbook, take behind-the-wheel lessons from an instructor, and practice on your own. And even after all that preparation, you may still flunk the driving test and have to go back for a second try.

When it comes to marriage, however, there's no official handbook, no marriage class at school, no dry run. For many of us, "marriage prep" boils down to an emphasis on planning the wedding and dreaming of a perfect life together. But once the big event is over and the newlywed bliss has worn off, we discover we don't have the tools to talk things out, or we're stifled by taboos and avoid discussing the important things that aren't working in our marriage.

Many people have the flawed notion that when we tie the knot all our relationship issues will magically be resolved. We believe that if one of us has irritating habits or we don't agree on certain things, the act of getting married will make all those problems disappear. Unfortunately, marriage doesn't stop dysfunctional behavior. It doesn't prevent harmful family dynamics, compulsiveness, addictions, depression, anger issues, or any other damaging behavior. It doesn't change the person. In fact, it can often exacerbate bad behavior over time because we may feel relaxed enough to let that part of us show. We can no longer hide the truth of our inner life from our partner. Then we're lost in a sea of regret, and the distance between spouses begins to grow.

ACCEPT THAT LOVE IS OUT OF YOUR CONTROL

When it comes to matters of the heart we can only stand in awe of the amazing things love can do. It can heal us and make us strong. It also has the power to bring us to our knees and challenge us to the very depths of our soul. If your marriage is ending or you've already signed divorce papers, you may feel unloved or unlovable. It is such an emotional time in our lives. When someone turns away from us for whatever reason even though we still want to be in the relationship, then we are going to go through many head-trips. Our inner life, memories, and conceptions about love are all going to surface, and we may find ourselves on our knees in pain. This is normal and to be expected. When my clients are going through these feelings of loss when a relationship ends, I remind them it is important to understand that we are powerless over people. We can't force anyone to love us. Love is given, not taken.

We are human. We are not machines that can be programmed to respond the way we would like each other to respond. The heart has a mind and a will of its own, and for many complicated reasons, we are not in control of who we love.

When we wed, we expect marriage to make us feel safe and secure. This is a beautiful concept, but we are never really safe from one of us having a change of heart. Just because we have voiced a commitment to each other, it doesn't mean we are protected from being abandoned or from falling out of love. What keeps marriages or committed relationships strong and connected is not a marriage certificate or the simple fact that we have taken vows.

The heart has a mind and a will of its own, and for many complicated reasons, we are not in control of who we love.

Think back to those vows. When we promised to love each other "'til death do us part," did we really mean that, or was it more like, "I will love you as long as you love me back as your romantic partner"? Perhaps a better intention would have been, "I love you, and I promise to give you my best and do the work with you to help each other to grow and stay connected. I am committed to working out the issues that come up between us and to continue to be self-reflective. I will focus on seeing my part in things and do the work to make the changes that are within my control." See examples of unrealistic and realistic vows below.

Unrealistic Vows

"I promise to love you 'til death do us part."

Realistic Vows

"I love you, and I promise to give you my best and do the work with you to help each other to grow and stay connected. I am committed to working out the issues that come up between us and to continue to be self-reflective and work on myself."

"I promise to approach our marriage from a loving standpoint and to work with you when challenges arise."

"I vow to be honest with you if my feelings change and to make an effort to address the reasons for those changes."

"I promise to treat you with respect even if we decide not to remain married."

In the face of heartbreak, it is critical to acknowledge that a marriage certificate cannot hold back the forces of nature. Think of how beneficial it would have been if we had paid attention to this when we entered into a marriage. Perhaps if we hadn't ignored the fact that humans are always changing, we could have made other types of agreements concerning our unions. For example, we could have spelled out guidelines for acceptable behavior and co-parenting in the event of a breakup.

Many business partnership contracts include terms for termination of the agreement so there are no surprises if the partners split. Why don't we do this with marriages? Yes, some prenuptial agreements outline financial arrangements in the event of a divorce, but they usually don't touch on behavior or post-split parenting styles. Instead, in the throes of a breakup when our hearts are broken and we feel destroyed and often times angry, it is very difficult to control our emotions, to think clearly, or to act compassionately. Our minds race to thoughts of revenge, blame, and retribution.

WHEN DIVORCE BECOMES A WAR ZONE

Custody battles. Alimony fights. Divorce pits us against each other, and it can begin to feel like we're in a war zone. The attitudes our society has normalized over time allow us to feel justified in our often-unfair treatment of not just our former partner, but also our former in-laws, extended family members, and even friends. Battle lines are drawn. Friends have to choose between the two people splitting up. Former in-laws get excommunicated. Long-term relationships are lost.

Our society gives others the right to make us feel like failures or bad people for going through a divorce. The way we collectively deal with divorce is archaic at best. At worst, it promotes shame, personal and social pain, and is extremely destructive to the families going through it. How we deal with divorce and blending our families has emerged as one of the most critical evolution points our society now faces.

Divorce is heartbreaking, but it is not a crime nor is it a declaration of war.

In a 2014 TED Talk, Danielle Teller, co-author of Sacred Cows: The Truth About Divorce and Marriage, revealed that two years prior to her divorce she had been diagnosed with breast cancer. She explained that when her friends and family heard the news that she had cancer, they dropped everything and gave her tremendous support, love, and guidance. But when she announced she and her husband were getting a divorce, she wasn't showered with love. In fact, the response was quite different, and she felt very alone.

The way our society treats people who are getting divorced is painful and detrimental on so many levels. Marriage is a beautiful concept and some people are lucky enough to remain happily together for a lifetime. Then there's the rest of us. For many reasons—some more acceptable than others—many of these unions end. This is not a crime. Divorce is heartbreaking, but it is not a crime nor is it a declaration of war. In fact, in many cases, divorce is the best decision for the health and well-being of the family.

Consider two people who fight and scream at each other and expose their children to a war-like environment all the time, but who choose to stay together and keep their marriage intact. They may believe divorce is a sin, or that the people in their families simply don't get divorced. Whatever belief system they have, they may think staying married no matter what is the best outcome even if they raise their children in a war zone or in a house where they live separate lives and show no affection to one another. Is that better than getting a divorce? Whether you stay together or get a divorce, what matters most is that you create a healthy living environment in which to raise your children.

What about situations where there is abuse, neglect, addiction, or serious mental illness? In these cases, a divorce could be a literal lifesaver. What about conscientious couples who have diligently tried to work through their differences but simply can't reconcile? What if one partner is intent on leaving, and the other can't convince them to stay? If you stay in the unhappy union, your family suffers. If you leave then you are divorced, and society says that is even worse.

Unfortunately, there is a stigma attached to divorce as there is on many other outmoded societal behaviors and rules. People who are divorced are not broken. This attitude needs to change. You do not have to view yourself as broken or lost. You do not have to accept the stigma placed on divorce. We can do better than this.

SHERRY: LOSING A VALUED RELATIONSHIP

Sherry, now in her mid-forties, lost her loving relationship with her grandfather after her parents divorced when she was twelve years old. Lines were drawn, and the two sides of her family were divided. Up until then, Sherry had spent her childhood with her big family celebrating many special events and holidays together. She was very close to her grandfather on her father's side. People even said they looked alike. He walked her to sleep when she was a baby. He was never too tired to take a turn pushing her on the swing or going with her for that last dip in the pool before dinner. He read to her, sang goodnight songs to her, and told her endless silly jokes and stories about his own childhood. As Sherry grew, he would tell her how special she was. He made her life sweet. They loved each other and were quite a pair.

When Sherry's parents decided to divorce, they were so hurt they stopped all communication with each other's side of the family. Sherry would still see her grandparents when she spent summers with her father. But things were different. Her grandmother would say little things about her mother, and her father would laugh and join in. Sherry's beloved grandfather tried to stop the mean-spirited comments for her sake, but he was overruled by the other family members and even accused of not being supportive of his own son. Sherry never really understood what had happened or why the dynamic had changed.

Things just weren't the same anymore, and she felt that maybe she had done something wrong to push her grandfather away. No one stood up and said, "Stop this insanity. They are family. They love each other. They aren't getting a divorce, you guys are!"

Her grandfather tried to bridge the gap with Sherry's mother, but he was rejected time and time again. When Sherry's father passed away, all communication with his family fell on her shoulders. There was no support for her. When her grandfather died, she didn't get to say goodbye. She had to ask permission from her own family to be allowed to see him and was denied by her own grandmother, who felt better about holding onto the grudge and anger the family had been carrying all these years. Grief-stricken, Sherry came to me seeking counseling. She couldn't sleep at night. She felt scared. She felt responsible for what had happened. This family was torn apart, and no one seemed to care about what was really important or how much heartbreak these lines in the sand were causing. Why would anyone want to do this to the ones they love? Surely it only added to the grief of the family. And Sherry will have to live with this for the rest of her life.

PARENTS OF DIVORCING COUPLES: A SOURCE OF COMFORT OR CHAOS

Parents of an adult who is going through a divorce can either provide support or can cause strife and destruction. Just think of Sherry's grandmother who, in an effort to show support for her son, cut Sherry off from her grandfather. This type of behavior is very misguided and can have devastating effects, as it did for Sherry and her grandfather. Not only did Sherry lose her relationship with her grandfather, but she also lost her ability to fall in love. When she did date, it was often with someone who was distant and not very nice to her. She modeled the behavior she had seen growing up.

When you are grieving the loss of your marriage and looking for comfort and support, an elder parent or grandparent can be a good place to turn. They can provide a safe zone where you can let down your walls and defenses, shed a few tears, and rest your head for a while. This is what it is like for a young child who takes a fall at the playground and looks up to see their dad racing toward them. The tears and emotions are unleashed as the child runs into Dad's arms in the hope of receiving unconditional love and understanding. In that moment the child does not need to be held accountable or judged for their actions. That may come later, but in that moment they need only comfort and reassurance that everything will be all right.

Elder family members who can offer this kind of nonjudgmental support can be key to coping with divorce. A true elder, a person of wisdom, will help to create calm within the family. When we feel heard and supported by our elders and are encouraged to be our best self, we know we are in good hands.

We were all taught to respect our elders, and when they are responsible in their care and communication with us, they deserve our respect. But some elders don't fall into this category. Some of them may judge you for your actions, question your decisions, or make you feel like you can't open up about your feelings. Some of them may demand authority, exert dominance, and stifle your opinions. It is very important in these cases to see that abusive behavior clearly for what it is and seek family support elsewhere.

GIVE IN TO THE GRIEVING PROCESS

Divorce is such a traumatic loss it can be comparable to a death. When we experience loss we grieve, but when we feel responsible for that loss we also punish ourselves as well as grieve. You wouldn't hesitate to take the time to grieve the death of a loved one, but if you are like many of my clients, you may not give yourself permission to mourn the loss of your marriage. Many of us ignore the human need to process our emotions in the face of divorce, especially when those feelings cause pain. Most of us try to avoid pain by distracting ourselves with work and the business of rebuilding our lives. But all this activity doesn't necessarily support our healing process.

When we stay connected it is an opportunity to give and receive compassion in a way that allows us to work through our grief.

We need to allow ourselves to take an emotional path through grief so we can deal with our pain, not just bury it. Some spiritual practices teach that in order to process pain, we must practice being with it, sitting with it, and allowing it to be a process rather than avoiding it, blocking it, or pushing it away. This requires time alone and space to feel our deepest connections to ourselves.

Preserving our connection with our extended family and circle of friends also supports a healthy grieving process. We are not designed to grieve alone. When we stay connected it is an opportunity to give and receive compassion in a way that allows us to work through our grief. Family and friends are so important to our healing process.

As hard as it may seem at times, we should never try to punish our spouse by withholding or destroying the community we both need. When one partner attempts to cut the other off from the extended family or circle of friends, they are actually obstructing healing. It is destructive to pressure family members or friends to choose sides or ask for others to refuse to speak to or see a former partner. This stalls the grieving process and perpetuates the pain.

HOW DIVORCE AFFECTS CHILDREN

Many unhappy couples are concerned divorce will have a negative impact on their children. But research shows divorce may not be as detrimental to a child's development as we think.

A study by Tamara Afifi, a professor in the Department of Communication at the University of California, Santa Barbara, uncovered some of the most compelling research discoveries of the past four decades regarding children and divorce. According to her findings, the true damage to children is caused by parental conflict more so than by divorce itself. Children whose parents have a lot of conflict and turbulence within the marriage, which creates a toxic home environment, have a far higher rate of long-term negative effects than children whose parents are divorced but are working together in a positive way to create a loving, supportive environment. The bottom line is that parents who fight in an unhealthy way impact the children whether they stay married or not.

These findings confirm that divorce is not always the worst thing for a child, especially when the parents are willing to work together to create a healthy environment. In some situations, divorce is a better solution for the children. Growing up with parents who fight or who stay with a partner even though they are miserable offers a poor example for children. Allowing children to witness a parent being mistreated can be detrimental to their development and warps their concepts about love and relationships. Children don't learn by what we say. They learn by example, by what we do. It's a given fact that some couples will divorce, and the children will be forced to endure the transition. For some, it will be a better situation. For others, it will be more challenging. Either way, the children need support. Everyone involved needs to give their best when it comes to the children.

> *These findings confirm that divorce is not always the worst thing for a child, especially when the parents are willing to work together to create a healthy environment.*

For this reason, it is critical to refrain from all-out war during a divorce. Regardless of how hurt you may feel, approach the situation with the best you have within and reach for your highest thoughts. If you do fight and yell and scream at each other, do your best to keep it away from your children and other family members. Make a vow not to drag your children, family, or friends into a war with you and your soon-to-be-former partner. It is extremely important to adopt a healthier approach to a divorce. You don't have to like it. You just have to do it. It is a behavior that is of service to the well-being of your children and your families. If you do feel good about it, that's wonderful, but it is not necessary to be happy about it. Be kind. Be gentle. Be calm. That's a good place to start.

HOW TO REMAIN LOVING AND CONSCIOUS IN THE FACE OF HEARTBREAK

If you find yourself in the position of getting a divorce, be aware there is a healthier way of going through it. With communication tools and better conflict resolution, you can heal from heartbreak and go on to have a happy, healthy, productive, and thriving family. With the following guidelines, you can tap into what is truly important as your relationship changes and discover how to deal effectively with the conflicts you are facing.

Try to maintain control.

Controlling yourself in the early stages of a breakup or during separation negotiations can be extremely difficult. I'm not insensitive to the immense pain you may feel if you have been betrayed, lied to, or abandoned. Your emotions may be pushed to their limit, and it will take a lot of self-control to maintain your balance during this challenging time. To help you navigate this fragile time, remember that you are in a position to have a big impact on your children's lives, your family's lives, as well as your friends' lives too.

Don't play the victim.

Even if the divorce is not your choice, and even if you feel hurt or angry, don't fall into the trap of playing the victim.

Take responsibility for choosing your partner.

Remember that you chose to commit to your spouse. By accepting responsibility you gain a sense of control over the outcome of your love life.

Take advantage of skills you learned in therapy or counseling.

If you and/or your spouse have seen a therapist, a relationship counselor, a spiritual practitioner, or some other type of supportive advisor, use the tools you learned from them. Allow this consciousness to be present as you dissolve your marriage.

Recognize if you need outside help.

If your partner is treating you and/or your family with disregard and unacceptable behavior, it is important for you to take a step back from the situation, acknowledge you are not in control, and reach out for help from someone who can help you stay balanced and empowered. Try to avoid surrounding yourself and your family with people who heighten the drama and contribute to a war-like environment.

Learn from what went wrong.

Make an effort to understand the reasons why your marriage is coming to an end and become willing to make adjustments in your own behavior going forward. If you don't learn from the mistakes in your marriage and you keep repeating the same patterns of behaviors, it is unrealistic to think you will have a different outcome in the future.

Accept that love is unpredictable.

The sooner you come to terms with the fact that love is not within your control, the sooner you can start to heal from the loss of love in your marriage.

Work through divorce as a team.

In this time of grief over the loss of your marriage, remember that your spouse has been your partner. Even if it is painful now, try to approach your divorce as a team. The time and energy you invest in rebuilding your partnership can help avoid damaging consequences down the road. Remember, by caring for your former partner, you are caring for your children's other parent, and this is a good thing.

DIVORCE DOs & DON'Ts

- Do create safe zones.

- Do separate anger and punishment from grief.

- Do talk to people who can support you in a healthy way.

- Do find the help you need outside of your family.

- Do accept that the heart has a will of its own and we are powerless over other people.

- Do learn how to regulate yourself.

- Do give yourself the space and time to grieve before you move forward.

- Do remember that life will go on and so will you.

- Do be gentle with yourself and others.

- Do go easy on yourself through the difficult process of divorce.

- Do respect those around you and treat them with care.

- Don't isolate yourself or your former partner from other family members or mutual friends.

- Don't create a war zone within the family.

- Don't ask people to choose sides.

- Don't hold yourself or your family to old, outmoded standards.

- Don't make divorce an excuse for bad behavior.

- Don't use your breakup as an excuse to fall apart.

NEXT STEPS

- Think about some ways you can prevent your divorce from turning your family into a war zone.

- Consider how you can maintain relationships with your former in-laws.

- Identify some family members and friends you can lean on for non-judgmental support.

- Give yourself time and permission to grieve the loss of your marriage.

- Think about how you can be more of a partner to your spouse during this process.

CHAPTER HIGHLIGHTS

- About half of all marriages end in divorce.

- As a society, we need to change our perceptions and standards if we are going to build and sustain a healthier generation of children who are growing up in divorced families.

- Many of us enter into marriage without a plan or any serious preparation.

- Marriage doesn't stop dysfunctional behavior.

- The heart has a mind and a will of its own, and for many complicated reasons, we are not in control of who we love or how we love.

- Divorce is heartbreaking, but it is not a crime nor is it a declaration of war.

- Research shows that divorce is not the worst thing for a child, especially when the parents are willing to work together to create a healthy environment.

- With communication tools and better conflict resolution, you can heal from heartbreak and go on to have a happy, healthy, productive family.

CHAPTER TWO

TRADE IN YOUR "ME-CENTRIC" ATTITUDE FOR THE SAKE OF THE CHILDREN

"I see children, all children, as humanity's most precious resource, because it will be to them that the care of the planet will always be left."
— *Alice Walker*

The truth is, when you have a child with someone, even if you divorce, you will be connected to each other for the rest of your lives. You will have to learn to co-parent and share in all the life events your child will go through. Even when they are grown you will remain connected because, hopefully, they will outlive you, and you will want to share in all the events of their lives and so will their other parent. I feel it is very important for us to accept and understand that when you have a child with someone, you will be connected for the rest of your lives even if you break up.

When you are parenting a young child while going through some of the toughest times during a breakup, you may not have the capacity to navigate the emotional ups and downs. You may feel lost or be so deep in grief or anger that you are not present for much else in your life, not even your children. You may develop a very "me-centric" attitude as a means of survival.

> *Contrary to popular belief, going through a divorce is not a license to act however you want in front of your children.*

During this time you may feel justified in being self-obsessed and out of control. You may lack your usual self-reflection and may temporarily lose your ability to self-regulate around your children. You may blame your harmful moods, words, and actions on your divorce. Contrary to popular belief, going through a divorce is not a license to act however you want in front of your children. And although it will require a good dose of effort to master some self-control, it is imperative to put your children first.

Think about how life shattering it is for a child to undergo a complete breakdown of the family unit. They are at the mercy of the adults making the decisions. And it is important to remember that they still love both parents even if the parents no longer feel that way about each other.

JANE AND HOWARD: LEVERAGING THEIR CHILDREN

When Jane's husband Howard left her, she was devastated. They had been having problems for a while, but Jane was convinced that their three-year-old twins would be the glue that would hold them together as a family. Now that Howard had left, however, Jane's anger and sad moods worsened, and she began unleashing negative comments in front of the twins. Although they were just toddlers, they could sense the underlying unhappiness behind her words. Meanwhile, Howard was MIA most of the time. He had moved into a new apartment and was working overtime to pay the bills.

The children began to act out, hitting and crying a lot when they were around other children. They got frequent colds and flu bugs and became fearful of going anywhere without each other. They developed a fear of dogs, water, sand—anything new or different. At both homes, they had trouble sleeping and became fussy eaters.

Jane blamed this on Howard and would say things to her children, such as, "Daddy left us, and he doesn't love us anymore" or "If you keep this up, I will leave too." Jane, who had a history of depression, would cry and hold them in her arms to comfort herself, saying, "Mommy needs a hug" or "Mommy is sad." She would call her friends and complain that Howard was a terrible man and that he thought the children had ruined his life—all while the twins were well within earshot. She began referring to the twins as her "ball and chain." Surprisingly, no one challenged her on this. Everyone felt so bad for Jane—not for the children but for her. Because Howard had abandoned her, they assumed this was normal behavior.

When Howard had the children on weekends, he would often say, "It takes me all weekend to get them to stop being so emotional and stop screaming and whining to get what they want." To cope, he gave them free rein to do whatever they wanted while they were at his place. He let them feast on ice cream, candy, and doughnuts. He allowed them to stay up past their bedtime watching movies. He took them to the toy store and bought them new toys. And they still had multiple meltdowns. At birthday parties, if the twins acted out, he would explain to the other parents that "their mother is crazy, and they are starting to act just like her." He said these things in front of the twins.

Both parents were leveraging the children to meet their own needs. Jane used them as an emotional crutch to help her survive the pain and sadness of the breakup. She was also subjecting them to "war talk"—negative comments that were distressing to the youngsters. Howard spoiled them as a way to deal with their bad behavior and wanted to be seen as the "fun" parent.

Neither Jane nor Howard had any inkling that they were the ones responsible for the twins' increasingly bad behavior. They were so blinded by their own personal emotions, anger, and frustration that they couldn't see what they were putting their children through. They were both so selfish and unable to regulate themselves that they didn't realize they needed to make changes to their parenting styles in order to make a safer, calmer, more stable home for their children. The twins' needs were being swept under the rug.

In truth, the twins were innocent victims at the mercy of these two adults who could not see past their own needs and justifications.

SEVEN WAYS PARENTS LEVERAGE CHILDREN DURING A DIVORCE

Like Jane and Howard, parents in the midst of a divorce often use their children as pawns in an effort to meet their own needs. In working with couples and families, I have identified seven specific ways parents leverage their children.

1. Using children for emotional support.

During a separation or divorce, many parents struggle to survive the upheaval and they turn to their children for emotional support. They negotiate the disruption in their life according to what they can handle rather than according to what their children can handle. I have worked with some very nice people who, in the midst of their divorce, could not find a way to put anything ahead of their own needs. Expecting your child to comfort you during your divorce places an unnecessary burden on their shoulders. Using them as a crutch for your sadness, pain, and anger adds to their discomfort. Leveraging them to fulfill your own emotional needs means you are likely neglecting their emotional needs. Using them, or expecting them to be a part of your support system, is unhealthy at best and deeply wounding at worst.

I am not suggesting you should act as if nothing is happening. Showing that you are hurt or sad in front of your children can be an honest exchange, but expecting them to make you feel better is taking it too far. In addition, if your former partner left you, and your children think you might fall apart emotionally, they may be worried that you will leave them too and then no one will be able to care for them.

2. Using children to punish or manipulate the other parent.

There are many ways parents use their children to get back at or to manipulate their former partner. For example, they may send mean messages on the shoulders of their children to each other. They may coerce their children into agreeing to be mean to the other parent.

One parent may refuse to allow stepchildren or half-siblings to remain part of the family hub in an effort to punish the other parent. Although this may have the desired effect on the other parent, it can also devastate the children and will tear apart the family. Withholding time and family from your partner by demanding allegiance from other family members is a sure way to create stress in your child's life. Expecting your children or family to choose a side or using this as leverage as a way to punish the other parent is going to create a war-like environment.

In my practice, I have also seen situations where one parent uses the child as leverage to elicit feelings of guilt in the hope of drawing a former partner back to the marriage. This puts the child in an extremely awkward position, making him/her feel responsible for the outcome of the marriage.

3. Using children to control money and finances.

I have seen families in which one parent basically uses the child as ransom to exact financial revenge on a former partner. Trying to drain the other parent's resources as a punishment for leaving, and justifying it in the name of the child, is very harmful to everyone involved. Making unrealistic financial demands can cause children to fret needlessly about their parents' ability to provide for them. The children may misinterpret the demands as a sign that their parents are suffering from financial strain. On the other hand, withholding financial support as a means to punish or control the other parent ultimately harms the children. Children need both homes to be solid and stable. If one parent withholds financial support as a means to control the other parent, they must realize their children will pay the price. The children have to live in that environment. As a parent, you want your children to be in a secure place and to have a warm, safe home. If that is not the case because one parent does not have enough money to take care of the things the children need, the other parent needs to step up and help the situation, if possible, for the children's sake.

4. Using children to appear responsible.

In some cases, one partner may strive to be the "fun parent." This parent isn't present for the day in, day out work of raising the children; nevertheless, he/she expects love, respect, and loyalty from the children and family. The fun parent often delegates to the children's other caregivers—the other parent, nanny, grandparents, older siblings, or friends—expecting them to enforce rules and boundaries. The fun parent may do this to gain a sense of importance or to prove that they are indeed fulfilling their role as a responsible parent.

On the flip side, one parent may assume all responsibility for the children, effectively shutting out the other partner when it comes to important decision-making and parenting. This creates an imbalance in the dynamics between the children and parents. Sometimes the more hands-on partner will leverage their self-imposed role as the responsible parent as an excuse for not being able to regulate their own life, mood, or temperament. The responsible parent may make excuses about being too busy with day-to-day parenting to deal with bigger-picture issues. In these scenarios, children may admire the fun parent while seeing the steadfast parent as a mean disciplinarian. Outside family members may also hold the hands-on parent accountable for any problems in the family. When children grow up, however, they will eventually see the picture clearly. In most cases, they will figure out which parent was there for them and which one really wasn't.

5. Using children to shelter yourself from stressful situations.

Many of the parents I counsel have disclosed that during the most painful times in their divorce, they hid behind their children to avoid awkward encounters. Are you sending messages through your child to the other parent or family members? Do you send your child to family events that you don't want to attend because they would make you feel too uncomfortable? Putting your child in these situations makes them responsible for things they should have no part in. Just imagine that if you, a grown adult, are too uncomfortable to have these conversations or to attend these events, it is exponentially more uncomfortable for your child. This type of leveraging can be overwhelming for a child.

6. Using children to stay connected to the other parent.

This type of leveraging occurs when one parent asks the former partner to get together for the sake of the children and then uses that time to manipulate and maneuver to try to work on the relationship. This can compromise the relationship with the children as they may feel there is always an ulterior motive being played out whenever both parents are present. A client of mine who grew up as a child of divorce recalled her mother using this tactic and said, "I just felt like I was being used as an excuse for her to get to talk to my dad about getting back together. I felt more alone, ignored, and neglected when I was with both of my parents than when I was with just one of them."

Expecting a child to act as a spy and to report back to you about your former partner's new home, new love interest, or new job is a form of emotional blackmail.

7. Using children to adapt so you don't have to.

When parents divorce, they are often so highly focused on their own needs and pursuit of their own dreams—a more fulfilling love from another person, a better-paying job, a more meaningful career—that they force their children to adapt. Children are forced to move back and forth between two homes. Children must adapt to two sets of house rules, two different daily routines, two sets of food in the fridge, and more. Adding pressure to their lives, it is the children who have to shuttle their clothing, personal care items, and homework between houses.

When children are hurting from their parents' divorce, it can be harder for them to think clearly and remember all these new rules and routines. Holding them responsible for forgetting to bring their favorite stuffed animal back to your home or refusing to go pick up something from the other house when it is really needed only punishes them.

GUILT, PARENTAL FLIP-FLOPPING, AND THE CYCLE OF DYSFUNCTIONAL BEHAVIOR

Leveraging isn't the only parenting issue that emerges in the wake of a breakup. Too many people allow their grief, hurt, anger, and other emotions to control their parenting, which can lead to unhealthy flip-flopping. One minute, you are feeling guilty so you overcompensate by spoiling your little ones with toys, gifts, food, or attention. The next minute, you are overwhelmed by their needs and punish them by ignoring them. This creates a lack of balance for the children, and a dysfunctional dependence starts to grow, leading to an unhealthy bond. You may wrongly interpret this dependence as a type of closeness and may protect it fiercely even if friends or family members point out the troubling pattern.

If you are like most parents going through divorce, you probably feel bad for your children, especially if they are struggling and acting in unacceptable ways. But feelings of guilt can drive even more dysfunctional behavior, not just from your children but also on your part. You and your children can hide behind the problems that come from a divorce so that none of the bad behavior actually gets addressed.

Instead, you may create stories to explain away the troublesome conduct. Then you address these stories rather than going to a deeper level and taking on the root problem. You may actively encourage other family members to participate in the stories you've created as a way to justify the questionable conduct.

In terms of the bothersome behavior, you may let it go as long as the good outweighs the bad. With my clients, I have noticed a number of reasons why parents avoid addressing the root problem. They may not have the capacity to deal with it. They may be afraid of a child's rejection or anger. They may be afraid of the feelings of guilt. They may be concerned that the core issue is too complex and involves too many people. They may not have the support of the other parent.

At some point, however, your offspring's behavior may hit the tipping point. You may be besieged with more bad behavior than good. At this point, you may try to enlist help from your former partner to tackle the underlying issue. In my experience, however, I have noticed that in this situation the former partner often refuses to help and instead defends the actions of the children. Without the other parent on board, it may seem too overwhelming to address singlehandedly, and you revert back to denial.

Unfortunately, by this time, it is often too late to address the problem on your own. Patterns are already deeply set, and it will take some outside help to heal the problem. It will also require everyone involved to emerge from the place they have likely been hiding for a long time—the land of denial.

You are not doing your children a favor by perpetuating the cycle of dysfunctional behavior. Others may begin to reject them due to their actions. They may misunderstand the rejection as jealousy or competition rather than seeing that their behavior is repelling people. This can lay the foundation for lifelong issues in the way your children relate to others.

CYCLE OF DYSFUNCTIONAL BEHAVIOR

- You minimize your child's bad behavior or deny that there is a problem at all.

- As your child's acting out intensifies and has more of an effect on the whole family, you finally accept that there is a problem.

- You feel so much grief and sadness about the behavior and think it is your fault that the issue becomes overwhelming and you switch back to denial.

- You create stories to explain the behavior and try to get family members to believe these stories. Anyone who doesn't go along with the act is targeted as being a problem.

- The child's bad behavior worsens.

- You try to enlist your former partner's allegiance to deal with the root problem, but this only activates the tendency for the other parent to defend the child's behavior.

- The lack of a united parental front causes so much additional conflict that you go back to denial.

By the time some of my clients come to me for counseling, they have allowed these dysfunctional behaviors to go on for so long that they have become solidified. Breaking these patterns requires a strong commitment and a willingness to examine your own part in the problem.

I have seen multiple generations of children who have grown up in families of divorce where the grown-ups felt so much anger and grief and had no boundaries on their behavior that it destroyed the foundation of the family. The healthy base was replaced with one formed out of dysfunctional behaviors and pain. Hurt and blame became the basis of decision-making and gave the parents and their children free license to act out. A routine part of daily life, this dysfunction became "normal" behavior and is now taught and passed on to the next generation.

Trying to help families address this behavior and introduce boundaries and understanding is often met with resistance. This is all the family has known and they cling to the guilt, pain, abuse, and negative talk because they see it as the family's bond. It is what ties them together.

With guidance, commitment, and effort, the dysfunctional cycle can be broken.

SOLUTIONS TO STOP LEVERAGING, STOP FLIP-FLOPPING, AND STOP THE CYCLE OF DYSFUNCTION

To put the brakes on the cycle of dysfunction, you need to stop the leveraging and flip-flopping and put your children first. Remember, even if they are acting out, they are not the cause of the pain. They are most likely reacting to the divorce and the unhealthy behaviors you and your former partner are displaying. It is your responsibility to protect them from the turmoil rather than embroil them in it. It is a tall order, but it is so important to consider when you are facing a breakup.

For the sake of the children, you must change your standards regarding what is healthy and acceptable for youngsters to endure. You can't just hold your breath and hope they will survive your breakdowns and come through the divorce unscathed. It is time to think again.

When you are in the process of getting a divorce, it is best to take an intentional approach to parenting. As you have seen in this chapter, parenting out of guilt and other emotions brought on by divorce can be very destructive and often leads to a cycle of dysfunction. The divorce is part of the problem, but it is not the whole problem. Whether you split up, stay together, live next door to each other, or reside in different states, it is not about the circumstance as much as it is about the behavior you engage in.

After years of working with families going through divorce, I've come up with the following solutions to help you shift your focus from your own needs to what's best for your children. Understand that you may never reach perfection, but even a little bit of progress will help. By holding yourself to a higher bar of behavior when it comes to raising your children, you may just help yourself in the process. Do it for the sake of the children.

Stop using children for emotional support.

Rather than looking to your children to provide support for you, it is imperative that you put their emotional needs first. If you are feeling sad, angry, or lost, keep those emotions in check while in the presence of your children. You don't have to pretend everything is wonderful; just don't burden your children with your negative emotions. As a parent, you need to learn how to "fake it 'til you make it." If you need to scream or cry, don't do it in front of the children. Don't do it in a way that brings them into a war. Talk to a therapist or a friend to vent your negative emotions.

Most importantly, make sure your children know that you are available to listen to them. If they are feeling blue, getting mad, or experiencing frustration, allow them to share these feelings with you without judging them. It is okay to let them know that you sometimes have those feelings too, but it isn't okay to make them feel as if they are responsible for your emotional well-being.

Remember, it is the parents who are getting divorced, not the children.

Stop using children to punish or manipulate the other parent.

Refrain from putting your children in the middle or using them to hurt the other parent. Your family will be much stronger if you do not draw lines in the sand and force people to choose sides. Your children need the extended family around them for support. Give them access to these people. Even if you are angry with these people, push aside those feelings and focus on the fact that they may be a comfort to your child. Help the children by creating a safe place where they can keep on loving both parents. Remember, it is the parents who are getting divorced, not the children.

Never use your children to manipulate your former partner by making them feel guilty about the divorce or trying to get them to move back home or call off the divorce. Keep them out of the adult drama. You are the grown-up, and these are grown-up issues. Protect your children from as much of the fallout as possible.

Stop using children to control money or finances.

For the sake of the children, both households must run as smoothly as possible and financial security should be a top priority. When both home environments are financially secure, it provides a sense of safety.

Stop using children to appear responsible.

Co-parenting your children is critical to their overall well-being. Make important decisions together and map out a co-parenting plan that you both agree to follow. Agree on similar house rules for both households, and stick to them. When both partners present a united front, it helps children find balance and fosters a healthy, functional family life.

"If anyone is going to be uncomfortable in the room, let it be me, not my children or my family."

Stop using children to shelter yourself from stressful situations.

As the adult in the equation, you need to deal with the pain and problems of divorce without forcing your children to face uncomfortable situations. Ideally, children want both parents to attend important events—school plays, sports tournaments, and graduations. As awkward as this may be for you, show up, act appropriately, and give your children as much support as you can. As I always tell my clients, my philosophy is, "If anyone is going to be uncomfortable in the room, let it be me, not my children or my family." After all, you are the one divorcing. Your children and family are only involved by proxy.

Stop using children to stay connected to the other parent.

Avoid using your children as an excuse to connect with your former partner. If you want to talk about reconciliation, say that. If you want everyone to be together for a family event for the sake of the children, say that. Don't say you want to do something for the children when that's really just an excuse for you to talk about getting back together. Don't ever put the children in the position of asking if you can join them on a visit or saying they won't go unless you get to come.

Stop using children to adapt so you don't have to.

Make the back-and-forth visits between parents' homes as seamless as possible. Create lists, have duplicates of everyday items, and take a more hands-on approach. Remember, the children's things are theirs, and you need to allow them to take what they want back and forth. Be responsible for helping them go between parents with as much flow and ease as possible. Do not use their things as a way to make a point to the other parent or show that you are more organized or responsible. Be their advocate. Help them and support them in feeling secure by managing the logistics for them and with them until they are old enough to do it for themselves.

Stop guilt-driven parenting and flip-flopping.

When you feel guilty about how your divorce may be affecting your children, don't overcompensate by spoiling them. Likewise, don't punish them by ignoring them when you are feeling overwhelmed. Consistency in your parenting approach is key to achieving the stability your children need.

Get to the root of dysfunctional behavior.

If your children are acting out, don't create stories to explain away their actions or pretend there isn't a problem. Make the effort to find out what's underlying their behavior and engage other family members to help address the root issues. This will be more challenging initially but will be more effective in the long run. Look to see what part you have played in helping to create the problems they are having and make changes in your parenting style as needed.

WATCH THE "WAR TALK" AROUND THE CHILDREN

My client Emma told her children, "Daddy left us. He doesn't want to be with us anymore. He wants to be with his new girlfriend instead." When Emma came to see me for counseling and told me this, I asked her if she had thought about how her comments might have affected her children. Surprisingly, she hadn't. Emma was a kind, loving woman, but in the face of divorce, she lost sight of how her words were impacting her children.

In my work, I have met many people like Emma, who consider themselves evolved in many ways and who are generally sensitive to others' points of view and needs. But in light of a divorce, it is as if a whole new personality emerges. This is especially true with people who feel blindsided by a partner's desire to divorce.

One mother, whose husband left her, proudly said to me, "My son won't speak to his dad. He is so mad at him for leaving us. He hates him." I was floored. I couldn't believe she truly thought this was a good idea to foster. From what she said, I could tell she was still hurting from the split. I hear these kinds of comments from many of my clients. I call it "war talk." And it can be very destructive.

When the breakup is not your choice, it is common to feel a range of hard emotions, such as abandonment, rejection, anger, fear, and shame. You may find yourself doing things that are uncharacteristic, such as saying hurtful things about your former partner in front of your children, who still love that person very much. By the same token, your former partner may be saying nasty things about you in front of them.

Words are powerful and can cause a lot of pain and confusion in children, who may already be feeling scared, angry, and confused. By spewing war talk around them, you are adding to the turmoil and causing them to begin to lose trust in their parents. The loss of trust is one of the key triggers of dysfunctional behavior. You must understand that when you are verbally attacking your former partner you are causing deep, lasting damage to your children. In my view, wanting your children to agree with your war talk about their other parent can be considered abusive.

You are an adult. You must stop yourself from saying hurtful things even if you are in so much pain that you can't stand it. Why is it so important to avoid sharing this negativity with your children, even if they are teenagers and seem to be angry themselves? You may be deeply hurt and angry now, but keep in mind that things will change, life will move forward, and relationships will evolve. The damage your negative talk will create, however, will last a lifetime. It will teach your children an unhealthy way to handle heartache and will diminish their chances of having a healthy, committed relationship of their own.

In addition, when your children grow up, chances are they will recognize how you talked negatively about their other parent and will resent you for it. Understand that the words you speak in times of crisis will become the wreckage you must deal with later, and sometimes the damage is so devastating it cannot be repaired.

Spare your children the mean thoughts. There are other places you can release these feelings. And whether you like it or not, it is important to not tear away at the fabric of the relationship between your children and their other parent. They are feeling enough pain from the situation as it is.

FLIP THE SWITCH ON WAR TALK

It is so important to watch what we say and do for the sake of the children. When you stop yourself from lashing out with war talk and start speaking with more compassion and understanding, you uplift the quality of life for your children and for the entire family. Remember that your children still love both parents. It takes a brave heart to admit this is true, so do your best to have a brave heart. In the long run, curbing the cutting remarks will benefit you and your children greatly. When your young ones grow up, they will understand that you took the high road and they will respect you for it.

If you aren't sure how to express yourself honestly with your children, consider speaking with a counselor or child therapist to outline what you will say. I help many of my clients learn a better way to communicate with their children. Take a cue from the following examples of how to shift from war talk to a healthy dialogue. Practice this type of phrasing when speaking with your children about your divorce, your former spouse, or your new living situation.

WAR TALK VS. HEALTHY DIALOGUE

"Daddy is leaving us." / "Daddy and I are separating."

"Your mom doesn't love us anymore." / "Your mom didn't leave you. You are always our child, and we both love you so much."

"Dad won't be around anymore." / "Your dad will still be your dad, and he will always be in your life. We will both still love and care for you together no matter what happens."

"I'm a mess. I don't know if I will survive this divorce." / "I will be okay, and so will you."

"Daddy didn't send the check this month. I don't know if we'll get by." / "Daddy and Mommy love you, and we will take care of these things. These are grown-up things that you don't need to worry about."

NO EXCUSE FOR BAD PARENTING

Sadly, our society condones a lot of the leveraging and war talk associated with divorce and allows parents to act out and then be forgiven for their horrible words and actions. Because divorce is seen as a failure—and sometimes a sin—the bad parental behavior that comes with it is too often tolerated and excused.

Our society supports the myth that if one parent leaves, they leave the whole family. This is wrong. Divorce is between the adults. It often has nothing to do with the children. But when a parent is supported in the idea that their partner left the whole family, that parent is more likely to lash out around their children and to use them to get back at their former partner.

The parent who has been left may think, "I'm hurt so you must suffer too." This type of thinking leads families into a war zone and contributes to dysfunctional behavior among the children. As a society, we may no longer justify this behavior of loose lips and leveraging. It is time to put a stop to these outmoded, painful justifications. We must create a safe haven for our children, not a war zone where they must choose sides. There is no side to be chosen.

Our society supports the myth that if one parent leaves, they leave the whole family. This is wrong. Divorce is between the adults.

As a parent, you should make it abundantly clear to your children that just because one parent left their spouse, they did not leave the family. It is the grown-ups who are no longer able to live together. Reassure the children that the love they feel for each parent is still reciprocated and the relationship between them and each parent is therefore strong and protected. Help your children to feel loved by both parents even if you are not feeling that yourself.

BETH, ROBERTA, AND BILL: CREATING A CIRCLE OF LOVE

When Roberta's mother, Beth, found out about her daughter's divorce she was really concerned with only one aspect of it. A strong supporter of her daughter, a doting grandmother to her three grandchildren, and a mother figure to her son-in-law Bill, Beth didn't want to lose any of these close, loving relationships. In a gentle way, Beth let her daughter know that she wanted to maintain her relationship with Bill as well as with her and the children. Roberta decided to trust her mother and work toward keeping the family as whole as possible.

What unfolded was gradual, loving, and unselfish. Beth remained a positive, steady presence in the family. Just as he had done during the marriage, Bill would take the grandkids to visit her whenever she needed help with household repairs or moving something heavy. They also stopped by just to say hi, which warmed Beth's heart. She would often invite them to stay and have dinner. The children loved this time and cherished the opportunity to tell their grandmother all about what it was like to live in two houses. Beth gave them her love and approval and also offered to help Bill with decorating his new place. She even gave him little family treasures that made his new house feel like a blend of the two families.

After a while, both Roberta and Bill met other people, and by this time it was so natural to be together that they continued including Beth in every aspect of the family. When Bill remarried, she was there with the children celebrating. When Bill's new wife had their first child, a son, Beth was honored as his grandmother.

Some things in life are out of our control, but in Roberta and Bill's case they conscientiously created a circle of love around their family. Because of this they were able to maintain a sense of belonging for their children and their grandmother. This didn't stop them from getting a divorce or moving on to other partners, but it did keep the breakup to what it was really about—the two of them, not their children or their family.

One added bonus, Bill's new wife, Holly, was thrilled to have Beth in her life because her own mother had passed away two years before she met Bill. Because of the decisions they all made together to let love come first, she now had a mother figure in Beth and her son had a grand-mother. The way this family approached parenting post-divorce has continued to help all of them work together to raise the children and care for each other as the years roll on.

PARENTING DOs & DON'Ts

- Do reassure your children that it is okay for them to tell you what they are feeling.

- Do tell your children that you will handle the grown-up things so they don't have to.

- Do act with kindness and dignity around your children.

- Do keep routines and family traditions in place as a way to provide continuity for your children.

- Do remember that you are getting divorced, not your children.

- Do act like the adult in the room.

- Do show signs of solidarity with your former partner so your children's world does not feel like a war zone.

- Do make time to have some lighthearted fun with your children, as it can be a relief to them.

- Do consider seeking counseling for yourself and your children.

- Do let your children spend time with both sets of grandparents.

- Do be prepared to pick up items your children forgot at your former partner's home, and do it with a smile.

- Do listen to others if they say they are seeing an out-of-balance relationship developing between you and your children.

- Do allow your children to grieve without feeling like you have to spoil them to lift them out of it.

- Don't put your children in the middle between you and your former partner.

- Don't use your children to send mean or negative messages to your former partner.

- Don't confide your hurt, anger, or despair in your children.

- Don't ask your children to choose sides—ever!

- Don't try to get your children to hate their other parent.

- Don't hold your children hostage by keeping them from their other parent.

- Don't make your children your new partner by leaning on them emotionally.

- Don't force your children to act like adults.

- Don't make your children feel afraid for your well-being or for their own well-being.

- Don't share with your children things over which they have no control.

- Don't talk about your negative feelings or anger when your children are present.

- Don't sugarcoat your children's bad behavior and compensate by creating a "special" dysfunctional relationship.

NEXT STEPS

- Recognize that you may have unknowingly leveraged your children.

- Think about how you can accept being the uncomfortable one in family situations so your children don't have to feel awkward.

- Take note if your children are displaying dysfunctional behavior and look for the root cause.

- Consider ways to give up "war talk" in front of your children.

- Find a supportive adult with whom you can "vent" your anger and frustration.

CHAPTER HIGHLIGHTS

- When you have a child with someone, even if you divorce, you will be connected to each other for the rest of your lives.

- Contrary to popular belief, going through a divorce is not a license to act however you want in front of your children.

- Parents in the midst of a divorce often use their children as pawns in an effort to meet their own needs.

- Too many people allow their grief, hurt, anger, and other emotions to control their parenting, which can lead to unhealthy flip-flopping.

- You are not doing your children a favor by perpetuating the cycle of dysfunctional behavior.

- With guidance, commitment, and effort, the dysfunctional cycle can be broken.

- Remember, it is the parents who are getting divorced, not the children.

- If anyone is going to be uncomfortable in the room, let it be you, not your children or family.

- When you stop yourself from lashing out with war talk and start speaking with more compassion and understanding, you uplift the quality of life for your children and for the entire family.

- We must create a safe haven for our children, not a war zone where they must choose sides. There is no side to be chosen.

- Our society supports the myth that if one parent leaves, they leave the whole family. This is wrong. Divorce is between the adults.

CHAPTER THREE

THE PROBLEM WITH PLAYING THE BLAME GAME

"We cannot solve our problems with the same thinking we used when we created them."

— *Albert Einstein*

Jill was shocked when her husband Brad left her for another woman. During their long marriage, they appeared to have a strong relationship. They went to church together every week with their four children and had a reputation in the neighborhood as a fun, loving family that did everything together. When Brad walked out, Jill was quick to blame him for leaving her for another woman.

As I grew to know Jill better, she began to open up about her life with Brad. She said that after their third child was born, Brad told her he didn't want to have any more children. He was hoping that one day after the children were grown, the two of them could travel the world together. What Jill told me next was eye opening. "I just went ahead, and even though he didn't want to, we adopted our fourth child," she said.

Jill didn't see anything wrong with the fact that she had not listened to her husband's request to stop having more children. She didn't think a major life decision like adopting a child needed to be mutually agreed upon by both spouses. In her mind, she assumed Brad would come around to the idea in time. It appeared that Jill had stopped listening to her husband and felt that she knew him better than he knew himself.
In reality, both of them had shown a lack of honesty. Jill initiated the adoption without Brad's consent, and he had not been more vocal about his feelings to put a stop to it. In the end, Jill felt like a deer in the headlights because she didn't see it coming and didn't understand his disconnect. She also made a joke to me about how he was traveling now with his new girlfriend.

In this case, Jill didn't honor Brad's request and didn't respect his desire to travel. In our society we are often encouraged to manipulate our partner or simply disregard their complaints and expect them to come around to whatever it is we want them to do. But trying to take control by ignoring, pressuring, or being too pushy or thinking we know better is a certain kind of dysfunctional domination.

We need to listen to our partners and honor, or at least recognize, their wishes. When this doesn't happen, we are setting up our relationships to fail. Jill didn't want to acknowledge this, and rather than examining her role in the disintegration of her marriage, she was stuck playing the blame game and pointing the finger at her husband.

WHY ARE WE SO QUICK TO PLACE BLAME?

When things go well, people are quick to take credit. When things go badly, however, people are less willing to take responsibility for the outcome. Instead they start pointing fingers at one another.

"Whose fault is it?"

"Who's to blame?"

"Who's responsible?"

"Are you willing to take the blame for this?"

These questions are so common we rarely give them a second thought. But the kneejerk reaction to place blame on someone or something whenever things don't go our way can be very damaging. In the case of the dissolution of a marriage or significant relationship, placing blame contributes to the creation of a war zone where sides are drawn. This represents a very dysfunctional unraveling of emotions and expectations. Yet blame speaks to some deep core issues within us that have been reinforced over many generations. Our families of origin, as well as current social standards, often allow us to justify ourselves through blame.

In general, there are many reasons why we may play the blame game when we are going through a divorce.

Blame absolves you of responsibility.

When you point the finger at someone else, it allows you to preserve your self-esteem while avoiding examination of your own personal failings.

Blame simplifies the situation.

Getting a divorce can be a messy, complicated process. Blame perpetuates the mistaken belief that a single person, decision, or event caused the problem at hand. Singling out one specific cause makes it seem easier to understand the dissolution of a marriage.

Blame assumes that outcomes only follow deliberate intention.

Pointing the finger at someone discounts the uneasy fact that some things are simply out of our control. Rather than grapple with this notion, some people find it easier to look for a cause and effect.

Blame requires little effort.

Accusing someone else is a way of allowing yourself to continue your behavior patterns rather than accepting fault or having to make changes.

Blame is a way to get people to take sides.

Blame can be used as a weapon to drive a wedge between your former partner and other family members and friends.

Blame lets you play the victim.

Assigning blame to your partner is a way to gain sympathy from others and can help you feel understood by family and friends. It also lets you justify your position in order to feel some relief and to get the support you need to move forward.

Blame satisfies a desire to find a right and a wrong.

Many people find comfort in the black-and-white concept that there is always a right and a wrong and that one side must be at fault or held accountable.

Blame makes you feel powerful.

Assigning blame to your spouse may give you the impression that you are taking action, which you may find empowering.

THE PROBLEM WITH PLACING BLAME

As I tell my clients, when you point your finger at someone else, there are three fingers pointing back at you. Taking a greater interest in placing blame than in how you can help yourself and your family deal with the pain of divorce presents problems. Here are some of the many issues with placing blame.

Blame is a distraction.

Blame shifts your focus from the true task at hand, which is to figure out how you are going to move forward as a family and get through a divorce. Making "who's at fault" the most important part of the journey prevents you from devoting your attention to creating a healthy post-divorce family life.

> *Blame shifts your focus from the true task at hand, which is to figure out how you are going to move forward as a family after a divorce.*

Blame is counterproductive because it renders you powerless.

Blaming others or circumstances is a way to avoid taking responsibility for our own life. When you blame, you abdicate control over what is happening and assume you have no power to change the situation. It prevents self-reflection and keeps you stuck in negative patterns. If you don't examine how you contributed to the problem, you are doomed to keep making the same mistakes.

Blame can be a cover-up for sadness.

Our rush to blame our former partner may be a cover-up for sadness. I understand that hearts are broken and that divorce can be catastrophic and that emotions about love and loss may be irrational. Our words and actions may be weapons we use to express our pain and anger at being hurt. The more we can get in touch with what lies beneath the blame and anger, the more we can find compassion and healing for ourselves.

Blame keeps you stuck.

Some people like to play the blame game because it makes them feel more powerful. Through my counseling practice, however, I have found that holding on to anger and resentment keeps people in bondage and keeps you stuck in patterns of bad behavior. If you don't own up to your own personal failings, it will haunt you and your future relationships.

Blame fractures families.

If you try to get your children to join you in blaming your former partner, you risk causing even deeper rifts in the family. Your children will eventually see through your attempts to manipulate them and may lose trust in you.

Blame perpetuates bad behavior.

When you blame your own bad behavior on your breakup, you are supporting it rather than addressing it, and this perpetuates more hurt and more damage.

Blame prevents healing.

Blame doesn't help save a relationship. It doesn't help you get someone back. It certainly doesn't help you mourn the loss or let it go. But the more important, deeper truth is that blame exacts a heavy price. Blame denies us the possibility to heal and to be emotionally free. When we don't take responsibility for our actions in the marriage, we tend to look for even more faults within our former partner's behavior. This makes us feel even less of a need to take an honest look at the marriage and our role in its demise. Without confronting the reality of what we brought to the table, we will not be able to heal.

SARAH, JOHN, AND WILLIAM: WHEN BLAME GIVES WAY TO LOVE

When Sarah was twenty-two, she had a baby boy named Nathan with her boyfriend John. Young and reckless, John made a lot of bad choices and wasn't there for his son or Sarah. Growing up, John never had a father figure in his life to offer guidance or to support the family. John's mother, Maria, had to work long hours to bring home food and pay all the bills. Sensitive and lonely, John turned to the kids on the streets for companionship and protection. As he grew up, he felt a bit lost. His behavior was often reckless and he got into trouble, a lot of trouble. Underneath all his bravado, however, was a gentle, loving young man who was learning things the hard way in the school of life. Even though he wanted to marry Sarah and be there for his son, his choices prevented that from happening.

Sarah saw that John was not ready for fatherhood and that it would be up to her to raise their son. In order to create some stability for herself and her son, she moved on with her life and started raising Nathan on her own.

A few years later, she met William, fell in love, and got married. William took on Nathan as his own son, and soon, Nathan had a baby brother, Paul. Around the time that Paul turned two and Nathan was turning six, John re-entered the picture. A little older and more mature, he had changed his ways and straightened out his life. He had a job with a delivery company, was living at home with his mother, and really wanted to be a father to Nathan. He called Sarah and asked if he could see Nathan and be a part of his life.

Even though Sarah had initially blamed John for his bad behavior, she was open to the idea. She wanted Nathan to know his biological father and knew how important that relationship was for her son. She also had a lot of compassion in her heart for John. She decided to speak to William about it to see if he would agree. William was the one who had stepped up to become the father Nathan needed, and Sarah wanted to treat him with the respect he deserved.

William and John both grew up in tough family situations, and they could have been very confrontational about Nathan. But William agreed to let John into the family and develop a relationship with his son. He made one stipulation: John could only see Nathan at their house while supervised until he proved to them that he was indeed a new man and could be trusted. And so the journey began.

When John would visit the house to see his son, Nathan's little brother, Paul, would be there too. Nathan called his stepfather Dad and his bio-father Papa, and eventually so did Paul. When John would ring the bell at the front door, Paul would run to greet him with his arms outstretched for a hug, shouting, "Papa! Papa!" The scene was moving for John and William, neither of whom had a positive father figure in their own life. The whole family could feel a sense of healing taking place.

With several successful visits under his belt, John asked if he could take Nathan home for the afternoon to spend time with his mother, Maria, who was Nathan's grandmother. Because things were going so well, Sarah and William agreed. When John arrived to pick up Nathan, Paul grabbed a little bag and started putting on his shoes. He wanted to go too. When Sarah tried to explain to Paul that only Nathan would be going, Paul whimpered, "My Papa too," and began to cry.

After Nathan had a few solo visits with his new grandmother, his three parents—Sarah, William, and John—decided that Paul would be invited on the next trip. Paul was so excited to go. He didn't have a grandmother who lived close by, so this would be a new experience for him. When they got to John's house, Nathan ran into his grandmother's arms and received a big hug. Paul stood waiting, but no hug was offered to him.

John's mother, Maria, was not open to loving a child who was not a blood relative. She felt that was asking too much. So the day went on with Paul following Nathan around, trying to get Maria's attention. A couple of hours before it was time for John to take the boys home, he received an emergency call from work. He needed to take over the last hour of deliveries for a driver who had fallen ill.

Because he was working really hard to keep his job, John asked Maria if she would watch the boys for that hour and then he would return to take them home. She refused. "I will watch my grandson but not this other boy, who is not mine," she said. John explained he was worried that if he didn't fill in for the sick employee, he might lose his job. Begrudgingly, Maria agreed, but added, "Only this once."

John headed out, and when he returned, he came through the back door, which opened into the kitchen. Thinking his mother would be angry with him for leaving Paul with her, John was shocked by what he saw. Nathan was sitting at the table eating the lunch his grandmother had prepared for him, and next to him was Maria with Paul sitting securely in her lap. When Paul saw John, he leaned back into Maria's arms with a big smile and said, "My abuelita." And that was that. Maria teared up at this unconditional love, and when her eyes met her son's gaze, they both knew that everything had changed.

From that day forward, Maria had two grandsons, Paul had a new grandmother, John and William both had two sons, and they all had become a blended family. It all started because Sarah was able to get past the blame, forgive John for his past problems, and see that he was making a concerted effort to be a good father. In this family, everybody won.

WHEN CHILDREN THINK THEY ARE TO BLAME

When children are involved in a divorce, they sometimes get the idea that they are to blame for it. They think they've done something wrong to cause the rift between their parents. Mom and/or dad, extended family, and friends may inadvertently reinforce this notion by engaging in war talk—negative comments aimed at the other parent or about the divorce—in front of the children. In some unfortunate cases, the parents actually do blame their children for the troubles in their relationship.

Children who think they are the cause of the breakup may also feel it is their responsibility to repair the relationship and save the marriage.

Whether they have been told it is their fault or they have come up with this idea on their own, children who think they are the cause of the breakup may also feel it is their responsibility to repair the relationship and save the marriage. If the parents are fighting, the children may act out and engage in negative behavior to draw attention away from the battle. They may try to manipulate the situation to get the parents back together. They may even get sick in an effort to stop the parent from leaving. When none of this works, it prompts them to place even more blame on themselves for not being able to fix the marriage.

Their efforts represent a desperate attempt to control a situation over which they have no control. When children think they are to blame, it can lead to long-term emotional damage and can make it difficult for them to bond in a healthy relationship as an adult. In addition, allowing children to carry this burden on their shoulders is unfair to them and can negatively impact the whole family.

KEEP CHILDREN OUT OF THE BLAME GAME

Don't blame your children for the breakup of your marriage and refrain from enlisting them in any efforts to place blame on the other parent. Using your children as pawns or putting them in the middle in any way wounds them. Be very clear with your children that pointing fingers or asking "who's to blame?" is not going to help them move through it. The truth is it will only help them feel more anger toward one parent over the other. Emphasize that what's important is moving forward as a family in a loving way. Reassure them that the breakup is not their fault and that it is the grown-ups who can no longer live together. Let your children open up to you about any feelings of guilt or responsibility, and offer unconditional support. Reassure them that you are there for them and that things will be all right.

Don't blame your children for the breakup of your marriage and refrain from enlisting them in any efforts to place blame on the other parent.

STOP BLAMING AND START REFLECTING

If you want to move forward and create a healthy family environment, you must forsake the blame game, engage in self-reflection, and own up to your part in the breakup. The sooner you realize this, the sooner you can experience personal growth, which will change your future and bring healthier interactions and relationships into your life.

Avoiding the blame game is not about losing sight of how hurtful breakups can be. There's no doubt that life is particularly painful when you are separating. You will grieve and go through a range of emotions. You may look at friends and acquaintances and feel envious, sad, or resentful because it seems like they have picture-perfect marriages. They don't. Nothing is perfect. A marriage may look perfect from the outside, but that's because you are comparing your insides to others' outsides. You cannot know the truth about another person's life or another couple's marriage.

To keep blame at bay, you can't make "who's at fault?" the most important part of your divorce journey. Eliminate the search for someone or something to blame. There's a saying—"different face, same issues"—that indicates we will repeat the same mistakes over again with our next partner unless we learn the lessons from our previous relationship. This is so true.

*A marriage may look perfect
from the outside, but that's
because you are comparing
your insides to others' outsides.*

Taking responsibility for your role in your divorce may seem like a more painful and difficult path, but it will pay off in the long run. It is so important to hold yourself accountable for your behavior around your children and family, who are innocent bystanders in your divorce. If you come from a place of self-examination and are willing to keep your side of the street clean and stay out of the blame game, you can create a safer, calmer environment for yourself, your children, and your extended family.

When you reject blame, you hold on to your power and leave behind the notion that you will die on this hill. You become a strong tree with deep roots. You become a safe harbor for your children. You teach them that you are not a victim, that you are present and accountable, and that you are working to grow and understand yourself and the ones you love. When you model this behavior for your children, you will find that they will treat you with a lot more respect.

As I tell my clients, it only takes one brave person to forego the blame game and adopt a healthier attitude. This can be enough to spark a small change in the family dynamics so that a positive ripple effect begins to spread. Let that brave person be you.

BLAME VS. COOPERATIVE COMMUNICATION

It is your fault. / Let's see how we can work together to improve the situation.

Mommy abandoned us. / Mommy and Daddy will always love you, but we are choosing not to live together anymore.

I'm so mad at you, I want the whole family to be mad at you too. / I'm very angry, but I will not try to get family members to take sides or blame you.

TRACY AND PHIL: UNDERSTANDING INSTEAD OF BLAMING

After nine years of marriage, Tracy was still in love with her husband, Phil. They were unusually compatible, and Tracy counted herself lucky to have such a good marriage. Although they were compatible, Phil had started feeling disconnected from their relationship. He told Tracy he didn't want to be married to her anymore and asked for a divorce. Tracy was deeply disappointed. Through her pain, she examined what had happened and came to the realization that she would not allow his rejection to reflect poorly on her personal value. She accepted that for whatever reason, he no longer felt she was right for him. She liked the concept of loving with open hands, and she felt if he didn't want to be with her then she wouldn't stop him from leaving. "If someone wants to leave, you don't stop them. Let them go. Trust that you will be okay," she said. Why would we want to keep someone by our side when they don't want to be with us?

The truth hurt. The loss hurt. But instead of blaming Phil or feeling resentful, she came to terms with the fact that she couldn't control love. And instead of creating false stories about Phil's inadequacy or trying to point the finger at a specific cause for the breakup, Tracy just felt sad. She turned inward and faced up to the fact that she was not perfect and that many of the issues between them had been real.

She let Phil know she was willing to work to overcome these issues, but he was not. He was ready to move on. Even in light of this, Tracy didn't blame Phil for not wanting to try. She consciously chose to respect his decision and love him with the same heart as always.

Tracy's choice to treat her husband with love and kindness even though he was leaving her is not the same as excusing bad behavior. Tracy was doing this for herself as well. It elevated her to a position where she was not dependent on Phil for happiness. Tracy exemplifies how adults can accept life on life's terms rather than only when things go our way.

What kind of love punishes us if we don't stay? This was one of the questions Tracy told me she would ask herself. She treated Phil as she would want to be treated. She said she had broken someone's heart before and understood on a deep level that if she went into blame and anger she would actually be hating Phil rather than loving him. Tracy knew that if Phil didn't want to be with her anymore she must not try to hold him by force. She understood the laws of love, one of which is that love is given not taken.

BLAME DOs & DON'Ts

- Do reassure children that they are not to blame for the breakup.

- Do take responsibility for your part in the breakup.

- Do recognize that you chose your former partner.

- Do be aware of the reasons why we may want to place blame when getting divorced.

- Do recognize the problems caused by placing blame.

- Do make your children—not the search for who's to blame—the top priority.

- Do remember that placing blame contributes to a war-zone environment.

- Do be aware of collective rage that has been passed down from one generation to the next.

- Do engage in self-reflection to own up to your part in the divorce.

———————— o ————————

- Don't blame children for your breakup.

- Don't let children believe they are responsible for your divorce.

- Don't let children think it is their job to help save your marriage.

- Don't let blame keep you stuck in bad behavior patterns.

- Don't try to get family members to side with you in blaming your partner.

- Don't jump on the bandwagon to create more pain by blaming someone.

- Don't condemn your partner just because past generations have carved out this pattern.

NEXT STEPS

- Think about instances when you may have placed blame on your former partner.

- Recognize some of the reasons why you may have resorted to blaming your former partner.

- Be aware of the problems that arise from placing blame.

- Consider what you may have done to contribute to the divorce.

- Take note of ways to incorporate cooperative communication rather than blame.

CHAPTER HIGHLIGHTS

- There are many reasons why we may play the blame game when we are going through a divorce.

- Blame shifts your focus from the true task at hand, which is to figure out how you are going to move forward as a family after a divorce.

- Children who think they are the cause of the breakup may also feel it is their responsibility to repair the relationship and save the marriage.

- Never blame your children for the breakup of your marriage and refrain from enlisting them in any efforts to place blame on the other parent.

- A marriage may look perfect from the outside, but that's because you are comparing your insides to others' outsides.

- Taking responsibility for your role in your divorce may seem like a more painful and difficult path, but it will pay off in the long run.

- It only takes one brave person to forego the blame game and adopt a healthier attitude.

CHAPTER FOUR

DATING POST-DIVORCE AND INTRODUCING NEW PARTNERS

"The meeting of two personalities is like the contact of two chemical substances: if there is any reaction, both are transformed."

— *Carl Jung*

AMANDA AND BRANDON: NEW LOVE LOST

Amanda had been divorced for three years when she met a man she really liked. Richard was easy-going and responsible, and he treated her with respect and kindness. Over the next several months of dating, they fell in love. When their relationship deepened, she decided it was time to introduce Richard to her son, Brandon. Amanda was so happy to be in love again, and she wanted Brandon to share in this happiness. She wanted their first meeting to be really special so she invited Richard to come over to celebrate Brandon's seventh birthday.

The meeting didn't go the way Amanda had envisioned it. Brandon threw a tantrum at his birthday celebration and flung his presents at Richard. Even though Richard stayed calm and didn't react to the outburst, Amanda was devastated. In order to get Brandon to behave, she told Richard he should leave the party. Amanda spent the rest of the afternoon trying to get her son to settle down.

The next time Richard saw Brandon, he got the same reaction. Brandon whined and cried the whole time in an attempt to steal Amanda's attention away from Richard. She couldn't stand seeing her little boy so upset and once again she asked Richard if he would go home. Amanda was still dealing with a lot of guilt about her divorce. Her family and society had reinforced those feelings, making Amanda feel like she had failed her son by getting a divorce. So she catered to him and let him dictate situations.

Amanda hoped Brandon would become more accepting of Richard with subsequent visits, but that didn't happen. Every time Richard showed up, it led to a meltdown. And each time, Amanda would cut the visit short to appease her son. Eventually, Brandon's actions and Amanda's inability to address them pushed Richard away for good. Now Amanda is lonely again and wondering if Brandon will prevent her from ever being able to have a lasting relationship with another man.

DATING AFTER YOUR DIVORCE

At some point following your divorce, you are probably going to want to re-enter the dating pool. Your desire for a romantic relationship will return. You may be thinking about yourself and your own desires for the first time in a long time. And when you do find love, it can feel like you are in uncharted territory where good judgment is no longer a prerequisite. You may find yourself acting like a selfish teenager.

But when you and your potential new partner both have children, it dramatically changes the dynamics. Dating after divorce presents many challenges, and you need to remember that children need and want grown-ups to act like adults. Even when you are in the rush of new love, try to stay focused on the things the children want and need—love, acceptance, belonging, connection, respect, and a safe harbor—as they try to navigate the effects of your divorce and the new structure of their life.

INTRODUCING A NEW PARTNER TO YOUR CHILDREN

Many of my clients ask me for help in navigating the difficult post-divorce dating scene. They aren't sure if they should talk about their dates with their children or keep it under wraps until a relationship gets serious. I usually tell them there are no hard and fast rules. Every family is different, and every situation is unique.

In general, however, keep in mind that after a divorce, children are often reeling emotionally from all the changes. They are likely being shuttled back and forth between two households. They are dealing with differing house rules. They may have had to change schools. They are likely wrapped up in all the emotional upheaval that accompanies divorce. Expecting them to weather the ups and downs of adult dating life on top of all that is too much and can lead to feelings of uncertainty and instability. For this reason, I typically recommend you keep the day-to-day excitement and disappointment of your dating life to yourself.

In my view, when you make the introduction to your children isn't as important as how and why you do it.

On the other hand, some children may feel betrayed if you bring home a new partner and announce that you are in a serious relationship. They may think you've been lying to them by not sharing that you have been dating this person for some time. It can seem like you can't win. So when do you make the introduction to your children?

In my view, when you make the introduction to your children isn't as important as how and why you do it. If you are in a situation in which your children will benefit from your involvement with your new love, you may want to step into those waters quickly, for example, after only a couple months of dating. In some cases, you may be more comfortable waiting for six months or so to see how your relationship develops. In other cases, you may feel that you want to be ready to be fully committed to each other before you involve the children.

Overall, if you can hold yourself to some healthy standards, you will be in the mindset to choose a time that allows the children to feel at ease and safe about meeting the new person. Make a conscious decision with your partner about how and when to make the introduction.

A lot of people make mistakes when it comes to introducing someone new to their children because they focus only on their own grown-up desires. For example, don't make an introduction simply because you want to see your new love interest, but you can't find childcare. This sort of behavior disregards the children's needs. You may try to pass off your date night as a fun time for the kids too, but it is really just you being selfish.

As hard as it may be, you have to do better than that now because children are involved. They need responsible parents who will make decisions with their best interests in mind, not people who can't control themselves or who put themselves first. Understand that this may get in the way of spontaneous romantic rendezvous or whirlwind weekend trips like you once enjoyed before you had children. As a parent, you may have to scour your calendars and schedule get-togethers weeks in advance around the days when neither you nor your date has the children or when you can both get a babysitter. It may feel as though some of the romance of a new relationship is lost due to the demands of parenthood, but you just need to accept this.

It is important to deal with the challenge of things moving a bit slower on the home front in order to let everyone adjust. Ease into spending time together until the two of you as a couple feel ready to bring the children into the picture.

When you are ready to make the introduction, keep it calm and easy and stay focused on the children. You can focus on each other when you are alone. Being inclusive and staying connected is a good balance. You want the children to see that you like and enjoy each other's company, but you don't want them to feel like there's too much intimacy. This can be confusing and triggering.

Remember, the children are coming from a position where they may be juggling a variety of emotions. Feelings about the possibility of their other parent being replaced by this new person could arise. This is a new playing field, and it is tricky for everyone involved. Be sensitive to that. Take it easy. Take it slow. Do whatever you need to do to create ease for the first meeting and beyond.

Here are a few practical tips I share with my clients to help make introductions to the children go smoother.

Don't make any big announcements on a first meeting.

When you introduce your new partner to your children, don't deliver any life-changing news, such as an engagement or plans to move in together. This can be traumatic for the children.

Go into it with realistic expectations.

You may have high hopes that your children will automatically love your new partner, but unrealistic expectations can lead to disappointment.

Keep it casual.

Forget the notion of planning a big event for the introduction. Do something low-key that your family enjoys—mini-golf, an afternoon at the beach, or a hike, for example.

Meet on neutral ground.

Rather than meeting at home where children may feel like the newcomer is invading their personal space, consider a location where they don't feel territorial, such as a park, the beach, or even an arcade.

Avoid holidays and special events.

A major holiday or family celebration can be one of the worst times to introduce a new partner to your children. Emotions—and anxiety, for some—are already high on occasions like these. Don't add to the stress by bringing your new partner into the mix.

Watch your language.

When you introduce your new partner to your children, avoid calling them your boyfriend or girlfriend. Call them a "friend" at first. After your children get to know the person better, then you can change to boyfriend or girlfriend.

Avoid overt public displays of affection.

When you first introduce your new partner to your children, skip the kissing and handholding. A quick hug hello or goodbye is okay, but overly romantic shows of affection may be too much for your children to process.

HOW CHILDREN REACT TO NEW PARTNERS

Children may react in many different ways when meeting the new person in their parent's life. Even within the same family, siblings may have very different reactions to the same situation. The important thing is how you and your new partner react to their reactions. For example, if your new partner shows up with balloons and smiles, expecting your children to jump for joy, they may be sorely disappointed if the youngsters run to their rooms to hide. At this point, it becomes about how you and your new partner handle the situation. Understand that this is a big deal for the children, and it is important to let them express their feelings. It isn't about pleasing the newcomer.

I've worked with clients who put their budding relationship ahead of their children's needs and got upset with them because they weren't accommodating to their new partner. Although I agree you need to set limits when children throw a tantrum or act out, and you don't want to allow yourself to be controlled by their behavior, you do need to listen to them. In this instance, you need to be the adult and act accordingly so the children get the message that they matter and that their feelings will be addressed.

When introducing your new partner to your children, be prepared for a variety of reactions and keep an open mind and an open heart. If you are aware of some of the most common ways children react to new partners, you'll have a head start in trying to help them work through their feelings.

Based on the stories of hundreds of my clients, here are some of the most common ways children react to a new partner:

- Give the silent treatment

- Be mean to new partner

- Feel like they have to be mean to new partner out of respect for their other parent/your former partner

- Blame new partner for taking attention away from them

- Feel betrayed because parent didn't tell them they were dating until it was serious

- Create chaos and throw tantrums to get parent's attention

- Be shy and clingy

- Be warm and open

- Act protective of their parent

- Have a strong need to control everything you do and how you do it

- Be happy to be a part of it

When introducing your new partner to your children, be prepared for a variety of reactions and keep an open mind and an open heart.

Before you react to your children's reactions, think about it from their perspective and understand that they are trying to navigate this confusing maze they are entering. They are facing yet another new situation in their lives by sharing their parent with someone they don't even know. They are trying to fit in to this picture rather than getting left out or being forgotten. Understand this and help them so they feel secure that they will never be left out. In other words, it is not a game for the children. It is real. If you are able to come from a place of honest intention to be there for the children and to be patient in introducing a new partner, you'll be moving in the right direction.

INTRODUCING A NEW PARTNER TO THE REST OF THE FAMILY

When and how to introduce your new partner to your family depends on your unique situation. If a significant amount of time has passed since your divorce, your family may be supportive of you dating and getting serious with someone. Your family may feel happy for you and will greet the new person with open arms. If the timing is good, they may see that you are happy and ready for a new relationship.

If you've just gotten through a divorce or breakup, however, and the family is still adjusting to the situation, it may be too soon to introduce a new love interest. They may question your readiness for a committed relationship, or they may worry that it is too soon for the children's sake. In some cases, the new person in your life may have played a role in the breakup of your marriage. They may have come along at a time when you had already mentally checked out of your marriage, and your connection with this person provided the impetus to end the unhappy union. To outsiders, however, it may seem like this person was a home wrecker and caused the marriage to fall apart. Family members may view the new person as the problem.

If you engaged in an affair with your new partner while you were still married, it could be asking too much from your family to accept this person right away. They may feel betrayed by your new partner and may be uncomfortable opening their hearts and homes to this person. There may be too much hurt and pain associated with this person, who may be seen as an intruder. In this case, you may need to wait for quite some time in order for the family to heal. Try to gauge your family's willingness to make room for the two of you before bringing your new partner into the fold.

Sensitivity is always called for because although you and your new partner have been bonding and growing closer, your family is still used to you and your former partner being together. This is not about asking your family for permission to move on, it is just about understanding and accepting that not everyone is going to feel the same way you do about your new relationship. Don't rush in and expect everyone else to understand how you feel. Take your time, stay connected, and remember that with time, your family will hopefully make a space for the new relationship.

Whatever your particular situation may be, the important thing to remember is that this is a time of transition for the entire family. Each person will be going through their own set of feelings, displacements, and struggles related to your new situation, and how they perceive it will impact them and their relationship to you and your children. Understand that bringing a new partner into this environment can cause more disruption. Keeping this in mind, be thoughtful about when and how you bring your new partner into the extended family fold.

DEVELOPING BONDS WITH NEW PARTNERS

When you've fallen in love with someone new, you hope your children and family will accept and even grow to love this person too. You might have a situation where your children are happy for you, and the new person in your life might fill an empty space for them and improve the entire family dynamic. I've worked with divorced people who met someone new, and it led to a healthier family. Their children received love and connection and a sense of belonging and importance from the new partner, which they didn't feel from their other biological parent. In these cases, it is a great, happy transition.

In most cases, however, there will be a few bumps in the road. There are always going to be challenges when introducing someone new to the family. Families are complex and have deep bonds, long-standing patterns of behavior, and unspoken familiarities. It will take time for the new person and the family to get to know each other. There will be an adjustment period for the two of you as well. You've probably developed your own routines as a couple, but now you need to weave those into the family fabric. It may take time for your partner to be accepted or welcomed in a capacity beyond being a stranger to the family. Accept that when you are blending personalities and dynamics it can be tricky and that taking your time and feeling ready is paramount. Don't rush it.

Rather than trying to rush or force a connection, what if you allowed your new partner and all the family members to move slowly toward a bond?

Some people expect a bond to exist naturally or to develop spontaneously. This may be in part because you are already feeling the bond with the new person and you want your children and family to be happy like you are. It may be due to the fact that you think this new person is wonderful, and you assume that everybody else will too. You may be hoping to create an image that "all is well" so your new partner can feel as if everything in the family is going great. You may try to rush things in order to make your new partner feel more comfortable with the idea of getting involved with someone who has an existing family.

Regardless of how wonderful you think your new partner is or how much you would like for that person to fit in seamlessly and feel loved right away, you can't expect your children and family to feel an immediate bond. It takes time.

The truth is meeting your new love can be a very stressful adjustment for children and family. When you are introducing new members to a growing tribe, there will likely be some conflicts. You may be triggered by some of the things others do and say. It may be hard on the new partner as well because they may not fully realize that they are stepping into a sea of emotions they didn't expect. They are happy. They are in love. They are excited. Then they meet the family or the children and aren't greeted with open arms, so they feel hurt and confused.

Rather than trying to rush or force a connection, what if you allowed your new partner and all the family members to move slowly toward a bond? What if you aimed for nothing more than basic acceptance and tolerance at first?

Doing so would require a healthy dose of patience, open-mindedness, and self-reflection from everyone involved. Self-reflection is one of the most important tools you have that allows you to be more honest about what is really going on inside and helps you see if you may be expecting too much too soon from your new partner, children, or family.

Don't confuse taking it slow with needing to seek approval from family and children. You do not need to ask their permission to be with someone. When it comes to your own love life, it is ultimately your choice. Just give it time. Wait until you feel sure enough about it to move forward.

WHEN YOUR FORMER PARTNER MEETS SOMEONE NEW

Finding out that your former partner has a new love interest can call up a range of unexpected emotions. You may feel sad, angry, or envious. If you are upset about this new person, share your feelings with a friend or adult family member with whom you feel safe to express yourself. If you hear the news from your children, don't lash out in front of them or expect them to comfort you. It isn't their responsibility. When there is another person brought into the picture by one of the parents, it is hard enough for the children to know how to deal with their own feelings without being fueled by the anger or sadness of their parent. If you can control your emotions in front of your children and help them to feel okay about what is happening, you will be doing them a great service.

If you don't have somebody new in your life yet, you may feel envious of your former partner. Even though you don't want to be with that person anymore, you may experience feelings of resentment, longing, and even regret. You may also be curious about this new love interest and how they are going to figure into your children's lives. Your first instinct may be to say nasty things about the new person in front of your children, or you may ask your children to tell you everything they know about them. These are bad ideas. Your children have enough on their plate. They don't need to listen to negative talk about someone who may end up playing an important role in their lives, and they don't need to feel like it is their job to spy on this new person or to answer questions about their relationship with the other parent.

If your children do choose to talk to you about this new person, don't repeat what they say to your former partner. This will erode the sense of trust they have in you. The best thing you can do is to create a safe environment in which your children can express whatever they need to say and know it will be kept confidential.

You are the grown-up in this situation. Act like it. Accept that you chose to have children with your former partner and that you are now divorced from that person. Their love life is their business. Do your best to create stability and balance for your children, not make things worse.

DATING SOMEONE WITH CHILDREN

When you start dating someone with children, you may be excited to jump in and become a part of their children's lives. Your desire to be included in all aspects of your new romantic interest's life might push you to want to be accepted right away. With this attitude, however, you may be in for disappointment or conflict. Allowing for things to happen in their own time and entering into this new situation with grace is the key. It is very important to take it slow.

Allowing for things to happen in their own time and entering into this new situation with grace is the key.

Understand that from the children's viewpoint, you are the newcomer. Although you and the children's parent are on board with this new element of life, they will need time to adjust and feel you out. You are not number one. They are.

Depending on the age of the children and the state of affairs surrounding the divorce, you will have a unique situation on your hands. Sometimes children will see a new romance in their parent's life as a threat, and they may be afraid of being pushed aside. A parent may be spoiling their children or overcompensating due to guilt from the breakup of the family. The children may be dealing with a parent who is leaning on them emotionally or trying to get them on their side against the other parent. The children may be under stress.

There are many things you will not understand until you have been around the family for quite some time. Understand that when you meet the children, you will be looking at them through the lens of your new partner, based on their biases and perspective. A clearer picture will emerge over time.

If you can be very, very patient and wait to be included and invited in by the children and other family members, this is the best approach. Offer warm easy help if you can, but don't take over or try to do things your way even if you are convinced that your way is better. If you feel the need to start controlling the children or thinking you will be the knight in shining armor who will fix all their problems, it could backfire. Try to be aware that there are many rabbit holes you could fall down. It might be a good idea to adopt some healthy boundaries so your feelings don't get hurt and you don't hurt anyone else's feelings.

Be aware that you don't really know what you are walking into, so tread carefully. This is different from not showing up or ignoring the children or wishing that your new romantic interest didn't have children. You are not dealing with an empty nest. If you don't want to make the effort to cultivate a relationship with your new partner's children, you should seriously reconsider dating someone who is already a parent.

If you move slowly and allow things to develop organically in your new relationship, there will be many gifts and joys to share.

TAKE TIME TO HEAL FROM THE SHADOW OF THE PAST

In order to allow for a healthy relationship with your new partner, you need to take time to heal from your divorce. Even in the best circumstances, however, healing can be limited by variables over which you have limited or no control, such as mental or physical illness, betrayal, or finances. Be aware that when you enter a new relationship, you may bring with you some of the wounds and patterns of behavior from your previous marriage and family. This can act like an anchor that weighs down your emerging relationship.

To remove that weight and create a foundation that will allow you and your new partner to grow, it is necessary to unravel where one relationship ended and the new one began. Recognize that due to past patterns and behaviors, you may find yourself inadvertently holding your new partner accountable for things they didn't do. Similarly, your new partner may hold you responsible for certain situations that aren't your fault. Try to recognize when the past is creeping into the present in ways that sabotage your new relationship. By identifying these patterns and doing the work individually to heal, you can adjust your response and expectations in relation to these triggers from the past.

Note that if you are involved with someone who has come out of a very dysfunctional relationship where there was quite a bit of emotional, verbal, or even physical abuse, it will be a challenge. Understand that it will require a lot of time and effort to work through the different layers that are being played out. It is not healthy to just accept the blame or adjust to the damage and adapt. This perpetuates the behavior and prevents either of you from growing or moving on from the painful past encounters. Then the damage compounds over time.

Take heart, there are ways to limit the damage from continuing into the future. A commitment to self-reflection and to doing individual healing work will really pay off. If you engage in self-reflection, which is a form of self-mastery, and then communicate your fears and feelings, it will put you on the road to healing old wounds and creating a higher state of awareness. You'll be raising the bar for both your lives.

WHEN A NEW RELATIONSHIP ENDS

For a variety of reasons, your new relationship may come to an end. Many of my clients have a lot of questions about how to deal with the end of a relationship when their children have gotten to know, accept, and care for this person. Should you encourage the children to stay in contact with the former romantic partner? Should you act as a middleman to facilitate this contact? Should you sever ties completely?

If you've been together for a significant amount of time and you and your partner have bonded with each other's children, it is very important not to disappear from their lives. It may be challenging to stay in their lives, but if you can work together with mutual respect, you can keep the ties that bind in place.

This can prove to be a valuable learning experience for the children. They may come to understand that love is not black and white, and that just because a couple breaks up, it doesn't mean they have to lose adults they have grown to love. The children can maintain a separate relationship with that person. As the biological parent, don't demand that your children give up a relationship just because you are no longer going to be with that person as a couple. Understand that there are new boundaries to be put in place and issues to be addressed, but if it was an important relationship in your children's lives, you should support them in maintaining that connection.

PEGGY AND DON: THE ART OF TAKING IT SLOW

Peggy and Don met through mutual friends and clicked immediately. They laughed and talked with ease and both knew right away that this was something special. Don asked for Peggy's number, and by the time she got back home, there was already a message from Don asking if he could take her out to dinner.

They had both been married before and both had children. Divorced for two years, Peggy had two children, Michael (nine) and Amy (six), who split time between two homes in a shared custody situation. Don, divorced for four years, shared custody of his eleven-year-old son, Rick.

In the early stages of their relationship, Peggy and Don went on dates when the children were with their other parent. Introducing the children to each other and creating an easy slow process of getting to know each other was very important to both Don and Peggy. They knew from past dating experiences that it was a rite of passage to be taken seriously.

They decided to meet on common ground out in the open where they could all feel comfortable. The introduction took place at a popular park near Don's home where Rick liked to skateboard. Michael and Amy brought their bikes, and they all just hung out and interacted in a very casual way. That first encounter went so well, they continued meeting at the park. When Michael and Amy tired of riding their bikes, they would watch Rick skateboard. When the ice cream truck pulled up at the park, they all ran over together and Don insisted on treating all of them. Then they would all sit on the grass and eat their ice cream cones together.

This scenario allowed the children to just be kids together. They didn't feel pressured to do or say anything other than they normally would with any other kids they met at the park.

In the beginning, Rick would sometimes rebel against spending time with Michael and Amy. He felt like they were too young for him. Don would remind Rick about how hard it was for him sometimes when his older cousins had left him out of games or ignored him because he was younger. Peggy would talk about growing up in an area where all the neighborhood kids played together despite the difference in their ages. Even so, Rick still chose not to join the younger ones from time to time. Don didn't make a big deal about it. Rick was allowed to have boundaries, and he moved at a pace that was comfortable for him. Every now and then Rick would bring a friend, and they would spend most of their time skateboarding together, and that was okay. On some occasions, Michael would tag along with them, and that was okay too. Rick slowly grew to like the fact that Michael looked up to him, and he would show off a bit in front of him.

Peggy made sure to thank Rick for helping teach Michael how to skateboard, and Don always took the time to acknowledge his son for his kindness to the younger ones. Don would express that he enjoyed spending time with Peggy and that it was so nice for them to be able to do things together as a group. Peggy and Don made sure not to overdo it with too many group outings at first. They made sure to continue having alone time with their children as well. They just moved slowly. Even though they wanted to be together all the time by this point, they waited until the timing felt right for the children.

Peggy and Don spent time focusing on the children, not each other, for the first few months when they were all together, and the children got used to it. Don and Rick helped Michael get up on his first skateboard, and when Amy wanted a go, they all jumped in to help her. Sometimes their visits would last an hour and sometimes a few hours. Don and Peggy let the children be the guides of these outings and never let the visits become too much for any one child. The focus was on creating familiarity without pressure.

On one summer night after a good long play at the park, Peggy suggested to her children that it might be nice to order a pizza for dinner and then she asked them privately if they would like to invite Rick and his dad back to join them. Michael and Amy said yes. This is how they began spending time together and it really worked for them.

Don and Peggy started being open about going out to dinner and a movie together, and when Don would pick Peggy up, he would arrive early so he could talk with and listen to the children before sweeping their mother off for a date. On one occasion, when Peggy announced that she and Don would be going out to dinner together that Friday night, Michael asked if Rick could come over. Peggy said, "Well, that's a nice idea. Let's call and see if he would like to come over and stay here with you and Amy and the babysitter while his dad and I go out." And that's how they eased into becoming a family.

By avoiding an awkward, forced first meeting, the children developed a bond with each other and with the new partner in a way that felt organic. Don and Peggy are now married, and the children like to say that they are the ones who brought their parents together. They know their parents had met before they all started going to the park, but they still feel like it was because of all the fun stuff they did together that caused their parents to fall in love and get married. In some ways, they are absolutely right.

NEW PARTNER DOs & DON'Ts

- Do take it slow.

- Do keep holidays and birthdays to family at first if that's what the children need.

- Do keep your opinion about your new partner's children to yourself unless specifically asked.

- Do be a respectful friend to your new partner's children.

- Do recognize that you are not their parent and that you must earn their love and confidence first.

- Do act like a grown-up and provide a good example.

- Do be willing to be on your own sometimes.

- Do prepare yourself for the many complex emotions children go through when a new person is introduced to the mix.

- Do try to build bridges not walls.

- Do reserve judgment of the former partner. You may not have all the information you need for a long time to realize what the truth is.

- Do understand that children may feel they are betraying their other parent by liking the new partner.

- Do understand you will never be a nuclear family.

- Do understand that it will take time to understand the whole picture, so be patient.

- Don't try to rush the bond.

- Don't demand respect from your new partner's children.

- Don't use the fact that you have someone new in your life as a weapon to punish your former partner.

- Don't date a divorced parent with children if you are not mature enough to be patient.

- Don't make your new partner choose between you and their children.

- Don't expect your new partner to take care of your children.

- Don't expect new partners to instantly love the children. Love takes time, and it doesn't always happen.

- Don't try to be their new best friend.

- Don't ask children for their opinion about your new partner.

- Don't get sidetracked by constantly thinking about your new love. It will cost you later.

NEXT STEPS

- Think about whether you have healed sufficiently from your divorce before you start dating again.

- Consider how you might introduce your new partner to your children in a way that doesn't put pressure on them.

- Recognize if you are trying to force family bonding with your new partner.

- Be aware of how you react to news that your former partner is dating.

- Give yourself time to develop feelings for your new partner's children.

CHAPTER HIGHLIGHTS

- Dating after divorce presents many challenges.

- In my view, when you make the introduction to your children isn't as important as how and why you do it.

- When you introduce a new partner to your children, they may react in a variety of ways.

- Be thoughtful about when and how you bring your new partner into the extended family fold.

- Rather than trying to rush or force a connection, what if you allowed your new partner and all the family members to move slowly toward a bond? What if you aimed for nothing more than basic acceptance and tolerance at first?

- Finding out that your former partner has a new love interest can summon up a range of unexpected emotions.

- When dating someone with children, allowing for things to happen in their own time and entering into this new situation with grace is the key.

- In order to allow for a healthy relationship with your new partner, you need to take time to heal from your divorce.

- In the event your relationship ends after you've been together for a significant amount of time, and you and your partner have bonded with each other's children, it is very important not to disappear from their lives.

CHAPTER FIVE

INTEGRATING FIRST AND SECOND FAMILIES AFTER REMARRIAGE

"Love begins at home, and it is not how much we do... but how much love we put in that action."
— *Mother Teresa*

In the United States, 75 percent of people who remarry already have children of their own. This means if you get married again, you are most likely going to become part of a tribe. You need to accept that once you make the conscious decision to remarry, you will no longer have an opportunity to have a nuclear family structure. You will be creating a tribe with stepparents, new siblings, and multiple sets of grandparents, aunts, uncles, nieces, and nephews. When you add more people to your family, you also expand the complexities of your relationships. As part of a tribe, you and your new partner will be faced with the challenges of integrating first and second families. In this chapter, you'll discover many of the pitfalls that come from integrating families, and you'll learn strategies to overcome them so you can create a healthier tribe.

CARMEN: FEELING LIKE AN OUTSIDER IN HER OWN FAMILY

Carmen grew up moving back and forth between two houses. Her parents were in their early twenties when she was born, and they did their best to stay together. But desire is not always enough glue to hold a family together, and shortly after Carmen turned a year old, her parents divorced. They each met new partners right away, got remarried, and started second families at the same time. Carmen talked to me about what it was like growing up as a first-family child in two second families:

> At my dad's house, it wasn't about the photos around the house or not having my own room. It was more about the subtle reminders that I wasn't a staple part of the family, that I didn't really live there and was mainly a visitor in my dad's family and home. Alternatively, at the home where I spent most of my time, I was far more rejected as a source of potential negative influence on my siblings.

In both homes, I felt I was the cause and source of frustration and friction. I felt I was the problem, and that was true, I was. I had nothing to do with creating that reality, not as a child. But I couldn't help but think that if I didn't exist, they wouldn't have to juggle me around or deal with my moods and issues. And I wouldn't be the constant reminder to my stepparents that my parents had a life before they came along.

It would have been better if my stepparents could have had a greater ability to feel less impacted. And I wish my parents had been more compassionate toward me and the situation they had put me in, rather than just thinking about what they needed to make themselves happy. I wish they could have known how I felt inside and if they could have sometimes, just sometimes, understood that when I got moody or acted out I was just trying to get the attention I needed to feel like I was important, rather than feeling like I was a pain in everyone's side.

As a child, I didn't know that being difficult made it harder for everyone to love me. I only saw that I got attention, and that's really what I wanted. If only they could have heard my silent scream for love and a sense of belonging, if only they could have thought about what I needed as a child, and if only they could have put aside their own needs and been more inclusive and helpful to me, things would have been much better for me and for everyone. I felt lost in their grown-up world. Now as an adult, I find myself still thinking, 'if only, if only.'

THE MYTH OF THE PERFECT SECOND FAMILY

Many of my divorced clients fantasize that their second family will be perfect. They have this notion that the problems they experienced in their first family will no longer exist in their second family. They feel like they've learned so much since their divorce that they'll be able to do it better the second time around. But there's a big problem with this thinking. The first family with all its imperfections still exists, continues to represent responsibilities, and will be forever intertwined with the new family.

I applaud my clients who have performed personal growth work as a way to improve future relationships. I encourage them to use their newfound skills and understanding to help heal the children they already have rather than waiting to put these skills to use with new children. Once you put dysfunctional dynamics in place between a child and a parent, you are most likely going to be impacted by them for the rest of your life. All your other relationships that involve the family will have to deal with it as well. This advice is often met with disappointment. It is understandable. People generally think it is easier to start over with a clean slate than it is to repair and deal with the decisions and behaviors of the past.

The first family with all its imperfections still exists, continues to represent responsibilities, and will be forever intertwined with the new family.

As you've seen in an earlier chapter, however, the saying "different face, same issue" applies here. Lingering issues within the first family that have not been resolved will continue to surface and will infiltrate and impact the second family.

Having a family is different than having a love affair. Romanticizing family is not a sustaining reality. Having a successful family requires investment, strategy, and prioritizing resources. If we all put as much intention into building our families as we do our romantic relationships, we would have much healthier tribes.

RUSHING INTO STARTING A SECOND FAMILY

If you've remarried and are considering starting a second family, proceed with caution. Parents all too often consider what they want as opposed to what their existing children need. The reality is that there are two sets of needs in first families: 1.) children who want stability and love from both parents and 2.) adults in crisis who are often driven by the desire for romantic love.

In defense of parents, they are often experiencing a deep pain that needs soothing, a pain that puts them in an altered state or survival mode that is essentially a selfish one. Second families are typically born out of these adult-centered desires as opposed to the children's needs. Consider that your first-family children are still in the process of healing from the divorce and probably need extra attention and emotional support. How will you be able to provide this attention and support if you add a baby to the family? Now is the time to examine what is best for the existing children.

Before rushing into the fantasy of a new perfect family, think about how the added responsibility will affect the family financially, logistically, and emotionally. Ask yourself the following questions to gauge if you are prepared for a blended family.

QUESTIONS TO ASK BEFORE STARTING A SECOND FAMILY

- Do you have enough living space in your current home?

- Are there enough financial resources to add second-family children without creating a deficit to the first family?

- How will you handle the age gaps between older first-family children and a second-family infant, who have radically different needs from their parents and environments?

- How are you going to deal with the dynamics of birth children in relation to stepchildren?

- Are you willing to sacrifice for all the children in the tribe or only for your biological children?

- How committed are you to making sure your children's brothers and sisters are all close and in healthy relationships with each other?

This list of questions may seem overwhelming, and it should. There are so many issues you'll need to address when integrating first and second families. It is precisely why I encourage my clients to examine their personal motivations before having children in a second family. What are your intentions and how will they affect the children who are already in your lives?

Unfortunately, the deep truth is that many people are unwilling to examine personal motivations and blind spots. That's why so many people don't choose new partners wisely and don't consider the consequences of their desire to have more children with a new partner.

Starting a second family without healing the existing family causes more damage for everyone involved. If you have one set of children who are already dealing with broken dreams and parents who are not getting along, adding a second set of children will only complicate matters.

When considering having more children with your new partner, realize that unexamined patterns and imperfections are compounded. For this reason, it is important to have a higher consciousness and to approach the possibility of a second family seriously. If a second family is not created mindfully, it will very likely place first-family children at a disadvantage, which can in turn impact the second family.

CHALLENGES OF INTEGRATING FIRST AND SECOND FAMILIES

As you integrate first and second families, be prepared to face some challenges. In a nuclear family, it is the natural hierarchy to have the parents as the authority and the children to follow. There is only one loyalty with one family. Once you create a second family, there are split loyalties and children are compromised. If you have a second family and all the adults are in alignment with all the children's needs, this hierarchy can exist with parents being the authority. But too often parents make decisions without considering anything other than their own desires. Consequently, chaos prevails and children are forced to adapt to situations that are in the best interests of their parents, not themselves.

This is often when dysfunctional behavior between a parent and child is born. Guilt for compromising the child sets in, and overcompensating becomes the parent's agenda. The child then grows up demanding to be compensated for what they lost along the way. This creates a dynamic that is problematic for the rest of the family. They too are expected to foster this relationship and give in to the demands of the dynamic duo or deal with the wrath of anger that ensues.

Understand that first families may still be under duress or in a compromised position following a divorce. It is common for first-family children to be experiencing difficulties from going back and forth between biological parents, being used as leverage by one parent, or being expected to provide emotional comfort for one or both parents. When a parent remarries, first-family children may be afraid that any new children will usurp their place in their parent's heart. Add in having to navigate new relationships with a stepparent and stepsiblings, as well as new homes and new house rules, and it can become overwhelming.

In my experience with my clients, I've found that most parents don't take the time or simply don't know how to help their first-family children navigate the transition. This can lead to even more problems for the first-family children. For example, they may start acting out and disrupting the second families. Due to the stress they are causing, these children may be left out of certain second-family functions and events. In some extreme cases, first-family children are completely excluded and not integrated into second families. More often, these children are subjected to more subtle forms of exclusion that make them feel like an outsider in their own families.

From the outside, it can appear that there is some justification for the exclusion. The children are seen as being "difficult" or a "bad influence" on their stepsiblings. But this is because the parent has not healed or has not allowed the children to heal after the divorce, thereby compounding the lingering issues.

When first-family children misbehave, it reinforces the perception that the first family is damaged. This becomes an opportunity to blame the first family or to label it as problematic. In some cases, this can lead to first families being dismissed or deprioritized as second families are established.

When first-family children misbehave, it reinforces the perception that the first family is damaged.

Other issues arise when stepparents resent their stepchildren because they represent a less-than-perfect situation and remind them of their partner's previous life and former mate. These parents often try to force the situation they wish they had and end up damaging the children in the process.

For many of these parents, the fantasy of the perfect second family becomes a fixation. Subconsciously or consciously, they try to push out whatever might expose or threaten that fantasy—usually the first-family children. They may reject them in an extreme fashion or in more subtle ways, such as displaying family photos that include only the second-family offspring, not the first-family children. Others might drop verbal reminders to the first-family children that they don't live in their house, that they are only visitors. In some second families, the parents may make it a point to recount family memories that don't involve the first-family children. All these methods are extremely hurtful to the first-family children and counterproductive to creating a functional blended family.

Just look at how this type of scenario can play out. During a family dinner involving all children from both families, one daughter from the first family starts throwing a fit. She is used to getting her way by manipulating her mother, who typically gives in to her demands out of feelings of guilt. The daughter doesn't get what she wants at the dinner table, and her deep need to control what is happening with her mother makes her lash out at the other siblings. In the heat of the moment, this dinner scene appears to be the problem. The mother blames the stress of the dinner rather than the out-of-control child and the dysfunctional dynamic she has created by systematically spoiling her and giving in to her demands. Meanwhile, the second-family children are upset by the attention and perceived protection the first-family child is receiving.

The result is that no one wants to go through this experience again, so the first-family child gets excluded from the next family get-together. The underlying dysfunctional dynamic remains unrecognized and unaddressed. So the situation perpetuates itself and worsens because the first-family child now feels excluded on top of everything else. The biological parent feels bad seeing the painful display by her child and tries to compensate by giving in or giving special attention to her daughter. As a result, the mother may exclude the new family, including her new partner, from interactions with the daughter from the first marriage. This creates an unhealthy sense of "specialness" for the mother and daughter, and it may become a pattern. Why don't parents want to address the root of the problem with the first-family children?

- Ultimately, the parents play a role in creating the problem.

- Recognizing the problem fundamentally confronts the parents as the source of the dysfunction.

- Even if the problem is recognized, the parents don't know how to fix it.

First-family parents may have deep-seated concerns that their existing children's needs will no longer be met or that they will be negatively influenced or hurt by the second family. Similarly, the offspring of the second family can feel competitive, especially if there are unequal parental bonds.

FAMILY OPERATING SYSTEMS

Every family has its own unique operating system, values, and daily rhythm. Integrating a first family with a new second family will require some adjustments. Think of it as part of the journey to understanding each other. And be prepared for some misunderstandings along the way. Sometimes simply doing or saying something the way it has always been done in your first family can anger, irritate, or hurt the feelings of a second-family member.

EXAMPLES OF DIFFERING FAMILY OPERATING SYSTEMS

- One family might wait until everyone sits down before starting to eat whereas the other family dives in right away because they don't want to let the food get cold.

- One family might be okay with yelling whereas the other family never yells.

- One family may expect the women to do all the housework and to prepare and serve the food whereas the other family may take a more egalitarian approach.

- One family stays up late playing games to enjoy time together whereas the other family likes to wake up early to walk the dog together.

- One family might acknowledge the need for privacy and personal space whereas the other family may not honor those boundaries.

No one system is right or wrong. Try to keep an open mind and understand that they are just different. If you are open to others' input, they may be more open to your input as well. If you all work together, you will eventually integrate the differences to create a new normal. Be aware that this will take some negotiation. Treating each other with respect is the key to successful integration of differing family operating systems.

DIFFERING HOUSE RULES FOR CHILDREN

As a parent, you'll have to adjust to different house rules and styles of discipline regarding the children. If at all possible, it is better to talk about these things before making the commitment to integrating two families. This is an area where it is important not to overwhelm the children or each other by making rapid, sweeping changes to the house rules. It is fine to make minor adjustments gradually, but they must be discussed and addressed together. Any rule changes should come from the parents as a unified front.

As the new boundaries, consequences, and expectations are put in place, however, it is normal for repercussions to arise. Be prepared for possible pushback, but vow to be consistent with the new house rules.

In some cases within a group of siblings, there will be a dominant personality who will demand to have things their way. This may create confusion, pain, and even suffering for everyone who has to change their ways to meet the demands of this person. This is not acceptable. One person should not rule the household. Be adaptable, and in time you may present your ways and even come up with new ways of doing things together as a blended family.

RECOGNIZE THE SACRIFICES CHILDREN MAKE

Family structure requires children to follow their parents' guidelines, live within their parents' financial means, and be dependent on their parents' ability to parent. They have no say in divorce or remarriage, although both affect them deeply and directly. As you restructure your family and house rules, consider that the children are the ones most directly affected by your choices and decisions.

Children should not be allowed to rule, but they do need to have a voice. They need to be heard and respected as individuals who are fundamentally affected by their parents' choices. You may feel you have a right to have your needs met and the right to remarry. You do. But consider this: children have the right to have their needs met as well. Children may feel they have the right to have both their parents remain together, but they lose that right when you choose to divorce and they are forced to sacrifice for your needs.

As you integrate your first family with a new family, keep in mind what I call "Children's Rights."

CHILDREN'S RIGHTS

- Children have the right to choose whom they want to love based on their own feelings, not because it is expected of them.

- Children have the right to voice their feelings about the changes in their lives.

- Children have the right to consistent parenting.

- Children have the right to feel included in a new family situation.

SUCCESSFUL INTEGRATION

In my work, I've noticed that the most successful second and third families have worked on integration while patiently respecting first-family children, prioritizing the care of all the children as a tribe, and giving everyone a voice. These families are not run by a dictatorship, but rather by a democracy, with team-centered practices. These homes incorporate rooms for, and mementos and photos of, every child.

Older extended family members are also integrated and encouraged to include all the children as their own. Aunts, uncles, cousins, and close friends are incorporated from first and second families and are encouraged to work together to support the children and the new evolution of the tribe.

It is important to keep children from feeling like they do not belong and to set the highest standards of inclusivity for all the children in order for the relationships to be whole and for families to thrive. The differences in values—cultural, religious, disciplinary—as well as the differences in ages and lifestyles are real, but they do not have to have a negative impact. Think of these differences as an opportunity for learning and understanding. Acknowledge the possibility that the second family can provide something additional that benefits you and your first family. For example, a new adult or new child in the family brings new strengths and gifts.

Second families must be an extension of our first families. If we choose to utilize the support available to strengthen the family structure, this provides new kinds of support in unexpected ways.

First, second, and even third families are part of the same tribe. This tribe supports and encourages inclusion rather than exclusion. This leads to more support, more accountability, and more guidance. We benefit by staying connected. You don't need to live together in a sort of commune or even live near each other, but you do need to live in connection and to acknowledge the extended family as a tool to make your lives better.

When first and second families work together to integrate, it adds more physical, mental, and emotional resources that can contribute to the tribe in powerful ways. We can find support in surprising places and in surprising ways that can enrich each other's lives. The more individuals who are involved in the raising of children or in the management of resources, the more those children and resources are protected.

NANA: A PIONEER IN INTEGRATING FAMILIES

My mother, whom we call Nana, is a true pioneer in the ways of integrating families. When my children's father remarried and had two boys with his new wife, Nana was filled with joy. She was thrilled to have two additional grandsons to love. The boys spend many afternoons at Nana's house playing—having cinnamon toast and hot chocolate on rainy afternoons and planting tomatoes and drinking lemonade during warmer weather.

Nana's house is a very special, safe, loving place where the boys know they come first. Nana benefits too. She gets to putter around in her beloved garden with her grandsons and play with them in the playhouse the same way she did when my children were that age. She gets to attend their school performances, help them make Valentine's Day cards, and teach them how to make mac and cheese. Being a grandmother of young children breathes new life into her.

As her family has grown bigger, she has rejoiced that there is more love to go around. Her family is thriving, and she feels abundant. She sets a great example for others who have expanding families.

Having Nana as such a strong pillar in our tribe benefits the entire family. My children's stepmother gets another elder to provide more love and support for her children. My grown children get to experience the joys of having their siblings around and get to share holidays and birthdays with them.

We have worked hard to integrate our families, and although it is far from perfect, our tribe is loving and inclusive. We work at it for our children, but we all benefit from it.

INTEGRATING DOs & DON'Ts

- Do realize that your decisions about your love life directly impact your children.

- Do make a commitment to integrate first and second families.

- Do ask yourself important questions about how new children would affect the existing children before starting a second family.

- Do be willing to let your first family heal from your divorce prior to remarriage.

- Do be prepared for the challenges that come with integrating families.

- Do be inclusive of all the children as you integrate families.

- Do allow children to voice their feelings.

- Do be aware that different family operating systems may cause confusion or hurt feelings.

- Do address changes to house rules together.

- Do be aware of the sacrifices children are forced to make.

- Don't assume your second family will be perfect.

- Don't rush into starting a second family.

- Don't require your children to call your new spouse Mom or Dad if they don't feel comfortable with that.

- Don't let first-family children be excluded.

- Don't use subtle forms of exclusion as a way to deal with first-family children's problems. Deal with the issues instead.

- Don't let bad behavior be an excuse to label the first family as a problem.

NEXT STEPS

- Examine your motivation for starting a second family and what the effects will be on your children.

- Think about how marrying someone with children binds you to them whether or not they bind back.

- Recognize that you and your children will have to make adjustments to your everyday routines and behaviors.

- Be aware that challenges may arise that surprise you.

- Give yourself time to heal your first family before starting a second family.

CHAPTER HIGHLIGHTS

- About 75 percent of people who remarry already have children of their own, which means if you get married again, you are likely going to become part of a tribe.

- You need to accept that once you make the conscious decision to remarry, you will no longer have an opportunity to have a nuclear family structure.

- When you add more people to your family, you also expand the complexities of your relationships.

- The notion of a perfect second family is a myth. The first family with all its imperfections still exists, continues to represent responsibilities, and will be forever intertwined with the new family.

- If you've remarried and are considering starting a second family, proceed with caution.

- Starting a second family without healing the existing family causes more damage for everyone involved.

- As you integrate first and second families, be prepared to face some challenges.

- When first-family children misbehave, it reinforces the perception that the first family is damaged.

- Every family has its own unique operating system, values, and daily rhythm. Integrating a first family with a new second family will require some adjustments.

- As a parent, you'll have to adjust to different house rules and styles of discipline regarding the children.

- As you restructure your family and house rules, consider that the children are the ones most directly affected by your choices and decisions. Children don't need to rule, but they need to have a voice.

CHAPTER SIX

ONGOING LIFE AS A BLENDED FAMILY

"To enjoy good health, to bring true happiness to one's family, to bring peace to all, one must first discipline and control one's own mind. If a man can control his mind he can find the way to enlightenment, and all wisdom and virtue will naturally come to him."

— Buddha

The challenges of life in a blended family don't end after the initial integration of first and second families. As you go through the years, you'll be presented with a variety of unique issues that nuclear families simply don't have to face. Parenting and stepparenting can get very tricky when you have your first-family children, your new partner's first-family children, and your shared second-family children, as well as both your former partners' second-family children and perhaps even some third-family children in the mix. Coordinating and collaborating with your former partner and their new partner in the parenting of your children can further complicate things.

For the children, having two sets of parents can be confusing. In addition, it can be difficult to manage relationships with full siblings, half-siblings, and stepsiblings of varying ages. Children may have a hard time finding their place in the bigger blended family. And as you've seen, the more people involved, the more complex it becomes.

Blended family events can often set the scene for dysfunctional dynamics. Finding ways to navigate it all while maintaining your values—and your sanity—is possible. But it will require consistent effort, self-reflection, and a commitment to putting the children first. In this chapter, you'll discover strong strategies to approach parenting and stepparenting, ways to help children cope with siblings, tips to help you survive family events, and more.

TAKE A CONSCIOUS APPROACH TO YOUR BLENDED FAMILY

As part of a blended family myself, I've learned it is best to take a conscious approach to life in a tribe. I've encountered all kinds of things that keep me growing and inspire me to turn inward in an effort to be more self-reflective. It is not always easy, and I'm sometimes shocked at how much I didn't see in the beginning. But over the years, I've realized that in our family, I'm but one leg of the table. I'm very important, but the other three legs are just as important for the table to be strong enough to hold all of us. I try to let everyone deal with what they are bringing to the table while I keep my focus on what I can bring. I've adopted a mantra that helps keep me focused. It works for me and for my family.

If I can remember that I'm not always in control...

If I can give others grace when I feel trespassed upon...

If I can forgive and allow myself to have healthy boundaries...

If I can forgive and allow other family members to have healthy boundaries...

If I can speak up when I need to speak up...

If I can listen to others when I need to listen...

If I can avoid rushing in and pushing my agenda...

Then the family will find its own balance.

I'm part of a parenting transformation that has been taking place over the past four decades. As a society, we are moving toward a more conscious approach to parenting. Roles have evolved, and mothers and fathers are consciously redefining those roles. Fathers are much more active in their children's lives. No longer is the father like some faraway male figure in a Disney movie, sweeping in to rescue his offspring from a forest fire and then disappearing again. Mothers don't always stay at home with the children and often work full-time. Some fathers are stay-at-home dads while some mothers are the family breadwinners.

In general, we are more inclusive of our children in ways that bring us closer to them and that make us more aware of and attentive to their needs. We no longer live by sayings like, "Children should be seen and not heard." We have a newfound respect for our children and allow them to have a greater voice in the family environment.

As first and second families integrate and we add more parents, stepparents, children, and stepchildren, isn't it time to rethink the internal workings of the family?

All of this amazing evolution around how to raise our children is wonderful, and yet it hasn't diminished the rate of marriages ending in divorce. As first and second families integrate and we add more parents, stepparents, children, and stepchildren, isn't it time to rethink the internal workings of the family?

When we come together with a new partner to create a second family, we have a responsibility to bring our best selves to the table. If we couldn't make the changes we wanted to make for ourselves, perhaps we can make them for our children. Sometimes this is part of the gift we receive when we are forced to change old patterns and bad behaviors we have carried with us for years. What we couldn't do for ourselves we can now do for our children. And everybody around us will be better for these changes.

What would it be like if we all came to this understanding and worked to self-regulate and to become more responsible? What if we decided to change our behavior and take a more conscious approach to parenting? It could change the whole playing field.

BREE: LONGING FOR A NUCLEAR FAMILY

A few years ago on Halloween, my friend Bree stopped by my house so her three-year-old daughter, Ashley, could trick-or-treat. Bree is someone I've always considered to be caring and thoughtful. She absolutely dotes on her child as well as her husband, Taylor, who also has a nine-year-old son named Miles from a previous marriage. As I handed some candy to Ashley, I noticed Miles wasn't with them and asked where he was. Bree said, "Oh, he's with his mother in his own neighborhood. We're doing Halloween just the three of us, our little family."

I was caught off guard by the comment, but I thought to myself that perhaps Miles wanted to be with his own friends who were closer to his age. But then Bree said, "You know, I just think it is really important to have time together as our little family and to make our own traditions with just the three of us." And then smiling, she added, "I don't always want to have him with us. You know what I mean?" She smiled at me again, as if wanting me to confirm her decision to exclude Miles.

I looked over at Taylor, who was looking down at the ground, holding their baby girl. I felt sick at the thought that he had to exclude his son in order to make his new partner happy. After all, it was Halloween. To me, that seemed like a good time for them to be together as a family unless there was an alternative family plan, such as Miles wanting to be with his friends without the younger one in tow. It seemed that he would be a bit young to be making a decision like that, and I was getting the feeling that this was an "I want to be a nuclear family moment" on Bree's part. I could see the confusion on Taylor's face. I knew that Bree meant no harm and that she was unaware of the impact her words were having on her husband. I wondered if she had thought about what it might be like for her stepson to feel like he didn't belong in his dad's new family.

She wasn't aware that she would never have a nuclear family, that when she married a man who had a child she had become part of a blended family. Her desire to create a separate family caused her husband to have to exclude his other child. It was as if she felt Miles wasn't part of their family.

I could understand her desire for a nuclear family. I see it frequently with my clients. But this is the kind of thing that really needs to be addressed before you marry someone who already has children. It is not acceptable to cause this kind of damage to a child by leaving them out of family activities. And it isn't okay to cause the father of that child to have feelings of guilt and pain.

I could see that Bree needed to understand that she should be letting Miles know that he was as much a part of the family as her daughter was and that he was always welcome to participate in family activities. If she wasn't willing to do that then she could be creating long-term damage and separation.

I hoped I would get a chance to provide some positive ideas to help her grow into her role as a stepparent to Miles and a strong hub of her blended family. Later in the week, I did have the opportunity to talk with her about it. She shared with me that her actions that night had caused some conflict with her husband, and she felt bad about it. In her heart, she thought she was doing a loving thing by creating family time for the three of them. They had a fight that night about something stupid, and Halloween ended up being a sad event for everyone.

When she asked me for my professional opinion, I carefully expressed my thoughts about it. She listened intently and was genuinely surprised at her lack of awareness about the needs of her new family as a whole. She couldn't believe she had been so insensitive to Miles and Taylor. The light bulb went off, and she finally realized she would never be able to have that nuclear family she had always dreamed of. She had a blended family, and she now understood that she needed to find the joy in that and she needed to nourish the whole family. Bree never excluded Miles again, and she made it a point to do as much together as a family as they could.

A few months later, Bree told me that being a blended family means just that. "We blend. We don't exclude," she said. "We aren't always able to do things together as a group since we share custody with his mom, but we always let Miles know that our family is not complete without him."

TIPS TO OVERCOME PARENTING AND STEPPARENTING ISSUES

When you have a blended family, you need to accept that you'll face a host of parenting and stepparenting issues that you wouldn't encounter if you had a nuclear family. After all, you may be in control of choosing your new partner, but you don't get to choose your stepchildren. Likewise, your new partner didn't get to choose your children. You'll likely be in for some difficult relationships in the family. As a general guideline, be aware of your own capacities and consider what you are able to take on, when it is best to take a step back, and where you are willing to make adjustments.

Spend one-on-one time with each child.

Whether you are the parent or stepparent, be sure to schedule individual time with each child so you can develop or strengthen your bond. Building up trust and your own special connection is important, so make the time and have fun. Keep it simple. Sometimes let the child take the lead and just listen. Show you care, and even if the child doesn't respond at first, give them time. Assure them that they are special to you. It is equally important that your new partner have individual time with each child. Don't feel like you need to join in every time your new partner is interacting with your children. Allow their relationship to develop.

Offer support on days when children go from one house to the other.

Every parent in a blended family knows that transition days can be stressful for everyone. Try to prepare ahead of time to make these days as painless as possible. The night before the transition day, offer to help the children choose their clothing or pack their bag. Ask them how they are feeling. Reassure them that you are always available to talk and be sure to check in with them while they are gone. On the day they return, give them some time to make the emotional transition. Be there for them when they are ready to talk, but don't expect them to jump back into the daily routine as if they never left.

Hold family meetings and let each family member voice their concerns.

Call a family meeting on a regular basis—perhaps once a week or once a month—and allow everyone to have a say. Let everyone know this is a safe time for any family member to talk respectfully about any issues. In my family, we have found that using a talking stick helps facilitate these meetings. Whoever is holding the talking stick has the floor.

Other family members must wait to speak or respond until they have the talking stick. You may find this method helpful or you may find something else that suits your family better.

Be aware of the strengths & weaknesses within the new blended family.

Build on the assets of the strengths that are already in place. If you focus too much on the negatives it will weaken the family structure.

Speak with respect about your former partner and their new partner.

As you saw in earlier chapters, it is very important to avoid war talk and placing blame around the children. Always be respectful and civil in front of the children and when in the company of other family members.

Avoid showing favoritism toward your own children.

When you blend families, you may feel a need to assure your children that they hold the most special place in your heart. This may be true because they are your biological children and therefore the bond is in place. However, fairness is a strong part of creating an environment in which each child feels loved in their blended family. Treat all the children as equals.

Avoid spoiling your stepchildren.

On the other hand, you may be so concerned that you will appear to be favoring your own children that you turn around and spoil your stepchildren. You may be doing this out of love, but it can be damaging. It is best to treat them all with the same level of love and care. Work together with your co-parents to create healthy boundaries and expectations for your whole family.

As a stepparent, accept that you may feel like an outsider at first.

Your new partner and their children will have routines, shared memories, and even inside jokes that you don't understand. Rather than feeling hurt or rejected by this, simply accept it and understand that it will take time for you to feel like part of the family.

Don't take on a disciplinarian role too soon.

If you try to take on an authoritarian or disciplinarian role from the start or are asked to take on these roles too soon, the stepchildren are likely to turn against you. At first, be more like a supportive friend. Be patient and work with your new partner to define your role and transition gradually to taking on a more authoritative, parental role.

Let the stepchildren decide what they call you.

Don't force the stepchildren to call you Mom or Dad, especially if they are older. If they are more comfortable calling you by your first name, let them do so. Over time, they may decide they want to call you Mom or Dad, and if they do, I hope for you, it will be a joyful moment in your life.

Create an environment of inclusion.

Ask yourself the following questions: Am I treating my stepchildren as my own? Am I treating the problems with each child the same way? Am I playing by different rules based on step versus blood relation? And regardless of what everyone else is doing, can I be the person to step up and create a safe and inclusive environment for all the children in my tribe?

Allow the children to love and be loved by all the members of the blended family.

A child can never have too much love. Allow them to share their happiness with any member of the extended tribe. Encourage and support children to open their hearts to love from their new family members.

Don't be afraid to ask questions or to ask for help interpreting something that's been said.

Misunderstandings are a great cause of stress and pain in blended families. We listen through a grid of our own experience, and what we hear might be something very different from what your new partner or your stepchildren intended to say. If you are taken aback by something that's been said, ask for clarification.

Bring your best, not your worst.

Often people are kinder and gentler with their friends than they are with their partners, children, or stepchildren. We sometimes do and say things to family members that we would never do or say to our friends. Think about what you are saying and how you are acting with your blended family.

Don't make the children choose between parents.

Show up with your new partner for your children's important sports games, recitals, school dances, and other events even if your former partner and their new spouse are there. Likewise, show up for your stepchildren's events even if their other biological parent is in attendance. On a personal note, my former husband and I made sure to be there for our children. It was one thing we got right during and following our divorce. It really warmed my heart when my daughter said, "I never had to choose between my parents. A child wants to have both their parents. My mom, my dad, and my stepmom were all there, always. I never had a birthday party or school event where all my parents weren't there together. It was always Mom and Dad. It was never Mom this year and Dad next year. I think that one of the best things my parents did was making it so I never had to choose."

WHEN THERE'S A PROBLEM

Even if you take a conscious approach to parenting and step-parenting and you follow all the tips to overcome common issues, you may still have problems with one or more of the children. This can occur regardless of a child's age, whether they are young or already an adult. In some cases, these issues may be temporary reactions to all the changes going on. In other cases, they may be related to unresolved dynamics from the first family. In any case, it will be critical for you and your new partner to come up with a unified plan to address the issue.

As a stepparent, your first reaction may be to ignore or avoid the child who is acting out. You may be tempted to point the finger at the stepchild and say, "I wasn't expecting this, and I'm not going to deal with it." But this is not acting like a partner, and it only adds to the problem. A stepparent needs to be part of the solution.

In some cases, you may come to realize that denial about the problematic behavior has been in place for a long time. As you saw in chapter 2, denial is the first step in the cycle of dysfunctional behavior, so it is critical that you acknowledge the behavior and that you both work together to address it.

There's a common saying: "Tread carefully when you're speaking to someone about their children!"

When a stepparent points out a child's problem behavior, their new partner—the biological parent—may or may not take the news well. The stepparent, in an effort to communicate and help, may end up stirring up emotions and forcing the biological parent to confront issues they want to avoid. It may lead to conflict between the couple if they aren't on the same page on how to deal with it. Or it could be the eye opener the biological parent needed to take action about a lingering issue. Sometimes having the support of a good stepparent as a partner can make all the difference in the family structure.

When there is a mutual desire between the couple to work through any dysfunctional behavior that comes up with any of their children, it can have very beneficial results for the whole family. As a couple, you need to decide if the stepparent and the biological parent are both going to be actively setting boundaries and consequences for the child's behavior. Alternatively, you may decide that the biological parent will take a more active role in addressing the issues while the stepparent steps back.

If you think that you alone can fix this child or this family, you're wrong. If you can't live with the fact that as a stepparent you have limited control, or you feel like you don't have the patience to deal with this dynamic, then perhaps you shouldn't get involved with someone who has children. Understand that we are "stepping" into a different role as a stepparent. We are adapting to what was created before we were part of this family. It's new, so relax and let the biological parent take a little of the lead as you get to know their children and their children get to know you. We need trust with our caregivers, and it may take some time to build this up within a new family. Let it unfold naturally over time. Let yourself have some breathing room too. Boundaries are good for all members of a family. Take it slow.

When there is a mutual desire between two partners to work through a child's dysfunctional behavior, it can have very beneficial results for the whole family.

Whichever route you and your new partner choose, maintain an emphasis on problem-solving communication and a continual willingness to experiment with new boundaries. There needs to be an understanding between the new partners that when you are dealing with a child displaying dysfunctional behavior, it isn't "you are with me" or "you are against me." You both need to respect each other's limitations and work together toward a solution. You may need to adjust your expectations so you don't demand more than what your new partner can provide, and vice versa.

If the child's problem behavior is a result of first-family parenting decisions, ask how you can work with the other first-family parent to help make the relationship healthier. By getting all the parents and stepparents involved in working toward a solution, you can help make progress. Always approach the issue by asking what you can do to make sure all the children are healthy and thriving. That should always be the priority.

If you find that the family is stuck in a pattern of behavior that just circles, it is time to ask for outside intervention from a counselor or family therapist. Sometimes these ingrained patterns are too deep to change without professional help. They may seem normal to the family members that created them and have been living with them for a long time. In this case, if you keep drawing attention to them without a therapist's help to intervene, you may be accused of being the problem yourself. And this could send you running for the hills.

BIOLOGICAL PARENT-STEPPARENT DYNAMICS

In many cases, tension arises from the relationship between a biological parent and a stepparent. Depending on the circumstances surrounding the divorce, people may have feelings of jealousy, resentment, or disregard when it comes to these relationships. When you are the biological parent, you have to learn how to co-parent your children with your former partner's new spouse. Just as you don't get to choose your stepchildren, you certainly don't have a say in whom your former partner marries, and you may not be thrilled about this person. Similarly, if you are the stepparent, you will need to interact with the individual who was once the most important person in your new partner's life. As you might expect, it can be tricky.

Accept that this is simply part of being in a blended family and accept the fact that you'll have to interact with this person. Show respect for this person and learn to communicate with them. Work together to present a unified front to the children.

*Work together to present a
unified front to the children.*

If you are the new stepparent and you are just getting to know the family, respect the rules of the parents when the children are in your care. Abide by their wishes regarding food, hairstyles, clothing, cell phone use, TV time, and more. For example, if biomom tells her tween daughter she can't have a cell phone until she's fourteen, but stepmom runs out and buys her an iPhone for her twelfth birthday, it is going to cause friction. If biodad is committed to keeping his two boys in the Boy Scouts, but stepdad isn't willing to drive them to any scout activities, it is going to be an issue. If you don't agree with the biological parents' rules, express your thoughts and see if you can all work together to reach a compromise.

SARAH, RYAN, JOEY, AND NATHAN: SIBLING STRESS

I know a couple who remarried and started a second family and now have twin four-year-old boys named Joey and Nathan. These rambunctious toddlers have two college-age siblings, Sarah and Ryan, from a former marriage. Although there is a big age difference, Sarah and Ryan want to love and know their younger brothers. The second-family parents began routinely demanding that the older ones babysit the twins or take them to the park for playtime. Every time Sarah or Ryan came to visit, the parents would use it as an excuse to leave so they could have a date night or run errands or go out with friends.

The grown children liked being around their younger siblings, but they were growing resentful that the second-family parents were making them take on a caretaker role with them. They wanted to have time with their parents too. They just wanted to be hanging out as a family. Because of this, the older ones started to back off from seeing their little brothers. They cut down their visits to the second family, and now they only see them on holidays. They have virtually no relationship with the twins now. And the twins are growing up without their siblings.

If the second-family parents could have recognized that they were putting too much responsibility on the older children, then they could have kept the sibling relationship stronger.

STRENGTHENING SIBLING RELATIONSHIPS

Siblings in blended families can be strong supporters and lifelong friends, or they can be a huge source of pain. When you are part of an extended tribe, you need to be prepared for a variety of common sibling issues that may arise.

Sibling rivalry:

Full siblings may band together to create a rivalry against their stepsiblings or half-siblings. It is the parents' responsibility to encourage their children to treat all their siblings with respect and love. Parents can set a good example by demonstrating love equally among all the siblings and including all of them in family events.

Privacy and personal space:

Children in new blended families may be asked to share a room with a new sibling. If they are used to having their own room, they may not adjust well to this change. If possible, let each child have their own room or at least someplace to call their own. I have known parents who converted a living room into a bedroom at night for themselves so their children could have more space. I know a woman who converted a second bathroom into a small bedroom for her toddler. She put some plywood and a crib mattress over the bathtub and was able for the time being to give the older child her own room. On the other hand, some children do well sharing a room. Just be aware of what their different needs seem to be.

Age differences:

When there are big age gaps between the children, it can be difficult for them to find their place in the new extended tribe. A child who was the youngest in their first family may now be a middle child and may not feel comfortable in that position. Older children may feel ignored if the new partners start a second family and are consumed with the care a new infant requires. Older children may resent you if you force them to babysit the younger children. Try to engage in a variety of activities rather than always catering to the more needy young children.

Make sure to schedule some special activities with just the older children so they don't lose out on those experiences with their parents because of the new, younger siblings. You need to accept that you will be going to movies, dinner, and perhaps camping with your older children and then have to do it all again when the younger ones grow up. Try not to ignore the needs of the older children. They deserve to have those age-appropriate experiences with their parents. Leave the younger ones at home and devote some special time to your older children, and vice versa.

Parents must make it a priority to help their children adjust to new siblings in a way that bridges age gaps and minimizes differences between blood siblings and stepsiblings.

Parents must make it a priority to help their children adjust to new siblings in a way that bridges age gaps and minimizes differences between blood siblings and stepsiblings. It is important that all the first-family and second-family children are able to integrate and that all children are treated equally. If there is a problem between any of the siblings, it needs to be addressed in a way that promotes equality among all the children. Treating them all as equals is central to the household's health. If the children are having a hard time adjusting to each other, consider taking them to a therapist who specializes in families and remember to go slowly. Rome wasn't built in a day.

MASTERING THE HOLIDAYS, FAMILY EVENTS, AND VACATIONS

In any family, holidays, birthdays, weddings, reunions, and vacations can be fraught with tension. In blended families, they can be downright chaotic. There is no time when differing family operating systems are more acutely felt and no time when dysfunctional dynamics are more likely to emerge. When you are a nuclear family, it is easy to feel like you are in control of things, such as where your family will spend the holidays or where you will go on vacation together. However, when you go into a second marriage or relationship—especially when there are children involved—it changes that dynamic. New family members and their individual preferences will need to be taken into consideration.

If you have family members who tend to control these events, it will take some new strategies and conversations to work through the conflicts that will arise. To save your sanity and keep the peace, you may need to take a step back and rethink how you approach family gatherings.

How will you spend your holiday? At whose house will you gather? Which family members will be invited? How many will come? What time will you gather? What food will be served? It may sound easy, but blended families may need to blend very different traditions.

Accept that families have different traditions.

Be aware that the traditions your first family cherished may not be ones your second family enjoys. For example, one family may gather at home for the holidays while the other goes on vacation. One family may spend the day cooking together while the other goes out to eat at a restaurant. One family may play touch football while the other watches an old movie. Acknowledging these differences is the first step to blending traditions and creating new ones.

Exclusion is out.

If you are thinking, "I want to spend this Christmas with just us and the baby" or "Can't we just be by ourselves this time?" the answer to these questions is no, absolutely not. It is cruel, exclusive, and unrealistic to exclude blended family members from your celebrations. When you chose to marry someone with children, you became a blended family and cannot eliminate or exclude in order to have what you think you deserve. No one forced you to get married. It was your choice. And in choosing so, you need to take care of the children first.

It will not always work for the whole family, which may now include many more people, to gather together all the time. However, it is the loving approach you take toward them that can make all the difference in the way your entire blended family will feel. Breaking off into smaller special groups or taking a "just us" sort of attitude is not a loving way to approach a blended family. It may seem special to have an intimate group, but if you are leaving people out and just being exclusive it can be hurtful.

Holidays are not the time to exclude family if you can help it. Sometimes families will naturally break into smaller configurations of the larger group based on where they live, or they might use the time to branch off and visit relatives they don't see often. There are many reasons why families may do things separately or at different times. What's important is that we handle feelings carefully and let others in our blended family know that we care and are connected even if we can't always be there in person. But nothing beats opening your heart and gathering your whole clan—or as many of you as possible—once in a while and celebrating your big blended family.

Stop controlling and start asking.

If you are used to being the planner and host for family gatherings, don't charge ahead with plans as if it is going to be the same way it has always been. Be sure to include other family members in the preparations and be careful how you communicate with them. Look at the difference between these two styles of communication.

CONTROLLING COMMUNICATION

We're having Thanksgiving dinner at our house. Will the two of you be joining us?

With this request, you may think you are being inclusive because you are making an invitation, but there is an undercurrent of control. You are actually dictating the plans. The family member on the receiving end can only accept or turn down the invitation. They've been left out of the original planning. This can lead to triggering people who are not used to being left out of family plans. In addition, if you haven't invited the entire blended family to your Thanksgiving dinner, it will force people to make choices between family members.

When you forget that there is a tribe to be considered you can get in trouble because you are really only doing what you want. If family members respond by turning down your invitation, it may hurt your feelings. You may feel rejected. You may not realize that by controlling the family plans, it may have hurt their feelings and made them feel rejected.

COOPERATIVE COMMUNICATION

We were thinking we would like to be part of Thanksgiving this year and perhaps even host it at our house. What do you guys think? What would you like to do?

This approach is inclusive in a way that allows other family members to have a say in the planning. It is a more humble platform for communicating. With this style, you are saying, "I respect that we are a growing blended family, and I am not a dictator. I realize I'm not the only one who has a desire to do things my way." By including others from the inception, you will create an inclusive energy that will become the basis of how your blended family operates.

Even with this cooperative communication, there may still be conflict. The families may decide to host separate events or split time between two households. The whole blended family may not be together the entire time. That's okay. Don't force it.

In general, you need to make a decision. You can plan your own thing and let go of the expectation that everyone else will attend. Or, if you want some or all of the relatives to show up, you have to plan it with everyone else.

This is why open communication and asking questions before solidifying plans for a holiday is important.

Be willing to negotiate.

Depending on timing, location, and availability, you may need to negotiate who will be invited to certain family events. Be aware of the feelings some family or friends may have if they are left out. As the family grows, it is often hard to accommodate everyone in the tribe at every event, so communication and understanding will be very important.

Negotiation will need to come into play if you have one large dominant family that tends to overwhelm and dictate plans based on size, power, and habit, and another smaller family that gets swallowed up or left out of the planning. A "my way or the highway" attitude will create conflict, so come to the table with willingness to reach a middle ground.

Consider trading places.

With holidays and family events, you'll need to learn to compromise. Maybe this year, you host the holidays at your home, and next year you spend the holidays at your new partner's parents' house or at their adult child's house. Be flexible and try to embrace new traditions.

Lend a hand.

When nuclear families gather together, there may be a system in place for who handles which chores. Maybe Dad made the turkey, Mom made the side dishes, an aunt brought dessert, and the children helped set the table. In your new blended family, those roles may not yet be defined. You may find that some family members never get off the couch or offer to help in any way. You may be surprised and annoyed when your new partner's children play a game while your children set the table. This can create conflict. Talk about the various chores associated with the holidays and decide together who will do what.

Set aside anger and rivalries for the sake of the family.

When family members harbor resentment or anger toward each other, it can complicate event planning. One of my clients told me, "My mother didn't come to my wedding, not because she had a problem seeing my father, but because my stepfather has such a problem with my mother being around my father. And even though she was not forbidden to attend, she knew the consequences would be high if she chose to go."

The fact that a mother didn't feel like she could attend her own son's wedding due to a family rivalry is incredibly sad. Are we so spineless that we can't show up and be kind for a couple hours? I urge my clients to stop being selfish, set aside their anger, and show up for the happy couple, or the college graduate, or the birthday girl or boy. The event is for them, not for you.

Accept that you may have to change your routines.

If you and your family are rooted in your habits and routines, you may have a hard time adapting to life in a blended family. Some of my clients have told me that vacations as a blended family have proved especially challenging. One of my clients said, "We went to a big theme park for our first vacation together as a big family. My kids and I wanted to get up early every morning so we could get to the park before the crowds, but my wife and her kids wanted to sleep in and lounge around the pool before heading to the park. We ended up getting to the park in the afternoon and then spent the rest of the day waiting in long lines. I was so angry, and my kids were upset because they missed some of their favorite rides because of the lines. I guess we should have talked about our daily plans before we left."

VIOLET: A HOLIDAY GONE WRONG

Violet was really excited about the first Thanksgiving she would be spending with her new partner Gabe and his family. She had three grown children, and he had two adult children and two young grandchildren. Violet was used to being the hub of all the holiday activities in her family, and she did exactly what she did every year—she planned the entire holiday herself and sent out the invitations to the whole family.

She was going to host the holiday in their beautiful home in a canyon area that's set amid hiking trails, horse ranches, and other natural wonders. In her mind's eye, Violet had it all figured out. The two families would merge seamlessly together and bond over long walks, horseback rides, campfires, and sumptuous meals.

Unfortunately, that's not what happened. Violet was in for a rude awakening. She became acutely aware that there were dynamics at play in Gabe's family that caused conflict and disruption. Gone were the long walks and horseback rides, and in their place were arguments and tension. Her new partner's family had other ideas about how they should be spending their time, and they did their own thing without consulting Violet, even though she was the one who had invited them into her home.

Violet was hurt by their behavior. She felt as if they didn't think she was important, and she felt railroaded. For someone who had always been her family's holiday and birthday planner, it was hard to accept. She had no idea that her new partner's youngest adult son was the planner in their family, and he took charge from the minute he arrived. Whatever this son wanted, everybody had to do whether they wanted to or not. Violet realized that Gabe's other family members would simply go along with the youngest son's wishes in an effort to keep the peace.

Violet had never encountered this family dynamic before, but it appeared that they had been dealing with this dynamic for years and were used to acquiescing to the youngest son's demands. There were a lot of unsaid, uncomfortable family mood swings going on. Violet found herself arguing with Gabe about it. They were not on the same page about how their family time should be spent or about how this one son was commandeering the entire family.

Violet finally had to accept that there were two families now, and they had very different operating systems. She realized that both she and Gabe needed to be willing to change the way they do things. Violet's ego was a little bruised, but she was willing to try something new in an effort to create some tolerance for each other so the scenario they had just experienced wouldn't keep happening or get worse.

Violet had to learn the importance of letting go of control. The gift for her was that she learned she could step back and take care of her side of the road. She could relinquish the idea that the entire blended family would all be together all the time for all the holidays. That was a big relief because hosting the holidays is a lot of work. Violet got her first taste of the freedom that comes with that.

She was also challenged to examine her motivation for trying to push the two families to bond immediately. She realized she needed to stop forcing it and let the family members take it slow. She focused on creating some healthy boundaries and found comfort in the idea that she could say, "No, thank you. I don't feel like doing that right now." And that was okay. She stopped feeling like she had to include everyone all the time. It meant a lot less work and stress, and it also shone a light on getting a little more consideration from the family if they wanted her to participate in something or to help.

Before that Thanksgiving, Violet felt it was her duty to host the holiday events and run around cooking and cleaning and making sure everyone was having a good time. Now she sometimes sits on the couch and drinks a cup of tea while other family members handle the cooking. And she loves it!

Violet is the first one to admit that their first Thanksgiving as a blended family was a fiasco. She felt like she was about three years old. Her feelings were hurt, she felt left out, and she was mad that everybody wasn't fulfilling her fantasy. But it was really eye opening to experience a new way to approach the holidays, to witness the blending of many personalities, and to realize and accept that she was clearly not in control. Violet realized the holidays would never be what they had been before becoming a part of a blended family. But she made a conscious choice to open her mind and accept the new holiday traditions they were creating.

BENEFITS OF A BLENDED FAMILY

There may be some hurdles to get through, but being part of a blended family can offer many benefits. As you work through the challenges, be sure to appreciate the joys too.

- You may enjoy the sense of belonging to a big family.

- Adding other members to an existing family often creates more balance.

- Children are relieved of emotional burdens when they see that their parents are happy.

- When children and parents are loved and taken care of, it provides a strong calming element for the whole family.

- A biological parent can feel good about being a blessing in a new way to their own children by creating a loving environment that feels better than the strained first-family relationship.

- All members of the blended family may feel a greater sense of safety and security.

- Children whose parents are remarried to wonderful new partners find that these people are a boon to their well-being.

- New partners who are stable and giving are a positive resource for the family.

- In an extended tribe, there are more hands to do the work of running a home and meeting the needs of the family.

- With more people in the family, children are exposed to more diverse knowledge, gifts, and talents.

- In an extended family, there are more relatives—aunts, uncles, cousins, grandparents—to love.

- Children may gain a mother or father figure where one was absent before.

BLENDED FAMILY DOs & DON'Ts

- Do stay open-minded and open-hearted and be willing to try new things with your blended family.

- Do be aware that you'll continue to face challenges and issues in your blended family on an ongoing basis.

- Do bring the best version of yourself to your new blended family.

- Do realize that family patterns established long before you came into the picture might take time to emerge.

- Do accept that you will have to co-parent your children with your former partner's new spouse.

- Do encourage children to develop and strengthen bonds with all their siblings.

- Do accept that family is not a popularity contest.

- Do take joy in the benefits of life in a blended family.

———————— o ————————

- Don't try to be the boss. Try to be a team.

- Don't make distinctions that create walls between biological full siblings, stepsiblings, or half-siblings.

- Don't focus too much on the negatives of a blended family life.

- Don't make decisions or changes in the children's food, hair, or routines without consulting their parents.

- Don't force stepchildren to do things your way if they are used to doing things differently.

- Don't expect holidays, family events, and vacations to be the way they've always been.

NEXT STEPS

- Consider if you need to take a more conscious approach to parenting and stepparenting.

- Examine if you tend to exclude any family members.

- Be aware if there are any ways you may be treating your biological and stepchildren differently.

- Ask yourself if there is anything you can do to improve your relationship with your former partner's spouse or your new partner's former spouse.

- Think about how you approach the holidays, vacations, birthdays, and other family celebrations and how you can make them more inclusive.

CHAPTER HIGHLIGHTS

- Life in a blended family presents a variety of unique issues that nuclear families simply don't have to face.

- As a society, we are moving toward a more conscious approach to parenting.

- As a stepparent, be aware of your own capacities and consider what you are able to take on, when it is best to take a step back, and where you are willing to make adjustments.

- Even if you take a conscious approach to parenting and stepparenting and you follow all the tips to overcome common issues, you may still have problems with one or more of the children.

- In many cases, tension arises from the relationship between a biological parent and a stepparent. Be open and make a decision to work together. There is no walking away because you are sharing children, so find a common ground.

- When you are part of an extended tribe, you need to be prepared for a variety of sibling issues that may arise.

- In blended families, holidays, birthdays, weddings, reunions, and vacations can be downright chaotic. There is no time when differing family operating systems are more acutely felt and no time when dysfunctional dynamics are more likely to emerge.

CHAPTER SEVEN

DEALING WITH DIFFICULT PEOPLE IN THE BLENDED FAMILY

"Love and compassion are necessities, not luxuries. Without them humanity cannot survive."
— *Dalai Lama*

"I have three grandchildren from my daughter. I'm very close to my daughter and my grandchildren, and my new wife is also harmonious in these relationships. Recently, my former spouse flew in to attend a birthday party for one of my granddaughters. She made such a big deal about not wanting me to be there that my current wife and I weren't able to attend the party. We became victims in order for my former spouse to feel comfortable in the room."

When one of my clients told me this story about his former partner, it led us into a discussion about how to deal with difficult people in blended families. I told him how common it is in blended families to have someone

who causes hurt and pain for everybody else and how often these disrupt-
ers, regardless of how out of line they may be, tend to get their way.

WHY DO WE LET THE MOST DAMAGED PERSON LEAD?

Why is it that so often we let the most dysfunctional person in the
family make all the decisions? Why do we let the most damaged ones
in the family take the lead? In most cases, it's because they are the ones
who shout the loudest, cause the most problems, and make the most demands. Everybody else in the family tends to do whatever it takes just to
appease them or shut them up because they would prefer to avoid conflict. Some family members may feel sorry for that difficult person or might
even blame themselves for their bad behavior. In some cases, feelings of
guilt may make family members overcompensate by giving in to the difficult person's demands. After all, the squeaky wheel gets the grease.

> *Why is it that so often we let the*
> *most dysfunctional person in the*
> *family make all the decisions?*

If we acknowledge there is a problem with a member of a blended
family—for example, a former partner, a young child, a grown child,
or a grandmother—then it requires us to follow through by addressing
the issue and doing the hard work to bring about positive change and
healing. But it is indeed hard work, especially when you're already dealing
with many other changes to the family structure. Sometimes it seems
easier to put on the blinders, go along with the status quo, and let them

act out. As you saw in an earlier chapter, however, allowing the problem to continue can ultimately create a cycle of dysfunctional behavior.

LOOKING BEYOND A DIFFICULT PERSON'S BAD BEHAVIOR

Finding out what is behind a difficult person's bad behavior is the first step to finding a solution. In my experience, I have found that difficult people tend to have issues with anger and a need for control. These may stem from deep-seated pain from past experiences.

Anger Issues

Difficult people typically have a negative relationship with anger. They may use anger to control, punish, avoid, dismiss, reject, or manipulate other family members. Others may lash back in anger. As a result, anger rules the room and creates an emotional emergency that requires immediate action. Like a fire, anger demands all the attention and resources of those in the room in order to extinguish it. Everyone has to scramble—internally or externally—in order to defuse the immediate threat.

Anger is dominant and overwhelming, and when it emerges, most of us just want to get out of the line of fire and typically will acquiesce to the angry person in order to avoid the conflict. When a person doesn't see how painful it is for others to be around their anger, it is difficult for them to understand the importance of learning to control it.

Sometimes one person's anger can become such a habit that even if they understand how destructive their anger is, they aren't able to control it. Anger is unleashed and then followed by an apology. This is an all-too-common cycle that can repeat over and over for years. It is also a behavior that, if not addressed, is at risk of being passed down from one generation to the next.

RANDY, TANYA, AND CURTIS: OVERCOMING ANGER

I worked with one remarried couple, Randy and Tanya, who had to deal with Tanya's former husband, Curtis, who had a serious anger issue. At family events, Curtis would rage at Tanya and their children then apologize profusely and ask for forgiveness. Tanya and the children would tiptoe around Curtis and give in to his demands just to make him stop railing at them. Randy confronted Curtis about the way he was treating Tanya and the children, and that just made Curtis even angrier. Fearing that Curtis would start a physical fight with Randy, Tanya begged Randy not to get involved. Curtis's behavior was beginning to create a real rift in their relationship.

With counseling, Randy and Tanya both learned how to create healthy boundaries and to limit how much Curtis's anger affected them. Whether Curtis was able to see that his anger was a major problem was no longer the main issue for Randy and Tanya. Having healthy boundaries became their most valuable tool and stopped Curtis from controlling things by getting angry. He was put in a place where he could no longer make the decisions for the family, and if he started to act out he was met with a strong boundary. Eventually, after a lot of threats and dramatic attempts to throw them off their boundaries, Curtis had to look at his behavior or lose the connection to the family altogether. No one was putting up with his bad behavior anymore. Curtis eventually connected with a therapist who helped him understand that one of the things he was lacking was impulse control. Once he began seeing his therapist regularly, his demeanor improved. He learned some techniques to calm himself. He put some tools in place for himself. The therapist also helped

Curtis learn to slow down and gain control of his emotions in situations where, in the past, he would have blown his top.

Control Issues

All too often, the difficult person in a blended family tends to be a controller. They need to feel like they are always in control—making all the important decisions for the family and telling everyone else what to do. They need to be in charge of all the family events—holidays, birthday parties, graduation celebrations, and so on. The first family may have given in to their demands for many years, so by the time a new blended family is formed the dynamic has been cemented in place. It can be very hard for the new blended family to deal with a controller. Setting boundaries and working with your new partner is key to changing a controller's behavior.

SARAH, JASON, AND GRETA: TAKING CONTROL FROM A CONTROLLER

My client Sarah had to deal with a controller when she got engaged to a wonderful man named Jason. They had both been previously married and each had one young child. Both of them were excited about starting their life together as a blended family. They wanted to have a low-key wedding at home, but Sarah's new mother-in-law, Greta, was a domineering controller, who insisted on taking over the wedding planning.

Sarah had thought that talking about the wedding with Greta would be a nice way to develop a relationship with her new in-law. But Greta immediately dismissed Sarah's plans for a small ceremony and began talking about hosting a big event at her country club. Greta told Sarah that a backyard wedding was "tacky" and that she would have to invite at least 100 family members. Sarah tried to interject, but Greta steamrolled the conversation.

When Sarah complained to Jason about his mother's behavior, he shrugged his shoulders and said, "That's my mom. You'd better get used to it." He explained that after his father died, his mother, who was only forty years old at the time, had been so lonely and despondent that she began micromanaging her children's lives. Jason said he and his two sisters gave in to Greta's demands because they felt sorry for her. The dynamic had now been playing out for decades and was firmly entrenched.

Sarah had never been faced with such a domineering force and didn't want to put up with it. It was her wedding after all, and she wanted to do it her own way. She was upset with Jason because he refused to confront his mother about her controlling behavior. Greta had dictated everything about their lives—which neighborhood they lived in, which house they bought, which preschool their son attended, which car Jason should buy, and so on.

As Sarah came to realize how much influence Greta expected to have on her life, she told Jason it was a deal breaker. Sarah would not allow Greta to rule her life, and Jason was going to have to help set boundaries to keep his mother in line. Reluctantly, Jason agreed.

Jason enlisted the help of his two sisters, and they slowly began the process of resetting the family dynamic. They went through counseling to learn how to communicate and set boundaries with their mother. They encountered pushback at first. Greta used her arsenal of emotions to get her way, which was trying and exhausting. But the family stayed strong and committed to making this change in all their lives, and eventually Greta stopped her constant hovering and started picking up some new hobbies of her own. She joined a gardening club where she met a nice man who became a loving companion. Greta started focusing on her own life rather than her children's lives. To her surprise, Greta discovered she liked it this way, and she felt a new freedom to do as she pleased. She felt healthier and happier, and that trickled down to everybody else in the family.

This shift wouldn't have happened if Sarah hadn't insisted that Jason make a change. Sometimes, it takes a new blended family member to point out that a difficult person's bad behavior is unacceptable and needs to change.

DON'T ATTEMPT A QUICK FIX

When you're dealing with a difficult person in your blended family, don't rush in to try to "fix" that person. If a person has been displaying dysfunctional behavior for many years, it's unlikely you'll find a quick fix. It may not be your relationship to repair. You can't change the difficult person and often you can't distance yourself from the problems they create. This may make you feel trapped or angry.

When you're dealing with a difficult person in your blended family, don't rush in to try to "fix" that person.

Oftentimes you'll find that you have become part of a triangle or, depending on how many family members are affected by the difficult person, a circle of dysfunction. There are so many issues to address, and it can be very draining, so choose when to step in carefully. Let the family members who are directly involved with the difficult person do the majority of the work of changing the dynamics within those relationships.

If changes aren't happening as quickly as you would like, give it time. Understand that sometimes people are working at their highest capacity and simply are not capable of doing more. Perhaps the best thing you can do is to lovingly support the family members in their struggle and acknowledge the growth they are making. You don't have to participate in events or show up for dinners if you feel uncomfortable. Sometimes the only option you have is to put some of your own boundaries in place. Oftentimes this will get the attention of others and they too will begin to set better boundaries around the difficult person or situation themselves.

ACCEPT LIMITATIONS

When you're trying to deal with a difficult, mean, or controlling person who disrupts the blended family, accept that all the people involved may have limitations that are keeping them stuck in the dysfunctional dynamic. If you keep running into a brick wall with certain people, try to look at it from a different perspective. Instead of holding them accountable for the grief and hardship they cause and expecting them to maintain the same standard of conduct as a high-functioning, evolved, mentally healthy person, consider the reality of their limitations.

When you're trying to deal with a difficult, mean, or controlling person who disrupts the blended family, accept that all the people involved may have limitations that are keeping them stuck in the dysfunctional dynamic.

Accepting that particular individuals may be damaged, fragile, or suffering from mental health issues is a better way to approach the situation. These real limitations may be out of their ability to correct at the moment. Even though the behavior is unacceptable, you need to acknowledge that you can't control it or change it. Getting angry or reactive just adds to the stress.

For example, if you keep asking a blind person to describe what color the wall is, you have unrealistic expectations. No matter how much you yell at them or how many times you ask the same question, you won't get an answer. The fact is that their vision is impaired and doesn't allow them to see. They're never going to be able to tell you what color the wall is, and you must alter your expectation of them, or you will just become angrier and more frustrated. This may seem obvious, but it is something to think about in terms of the difficult person.

When someone has limited abilities don't let them be in control of things—ever. There is a choice to be made for the safety of all concerned. For example, if a child is unable to understand the rules of the road and the complexities of driving a car, we don't put them behind the wheel and say, "Let's go." It is the same with being a healthy, rational, and balanced person. These kinds of people get to make decisions and choose things that may affect the whole family, but if a person is unbalanced or out of control, they lose that position because they cannot be trusted to make good, sound decisions.

Consider if they might have a mental health disorder, such as bipolar disorder, narcissism, or depression. If you knew they had a mental health disorder, would it change what you expect from them? What if you knew they were deeply wounded by past experiences? Would that alter your expectations? What if you could put the difficult person into a category called "the most damaged person in the room"?

By acknowledging their limitations, you can remove some of the power they hold over you or at least minimize how much of your serenity you allow them to take from you. Here are some additional tips to help you work within people's limitations.

Know your audience.

Try to see beyond their bad behavior to understand why they are acting the way they do. Speak to them in terms they can relate to.

Stop trying to force them to do what you want.

Don't expect more from the person than they are capable of giving.

Recognize the other person's pain.

Understand that this person's actions and words come from a place of pain. Think about how you can help provide a solution to their pain rather than adding to it, even if that means limiting your interactions with them.

Accept your own limitations.

When you're dealing with a difficult person, you need to accept not only their limitations but also your own. Recognize that you may not be emotionally equipped or may not have the tools to address the issues that contribute to their behavior. Set boundaries and make plans that provide you some distance from the conflict. Consult with a counselor or family therapist to assist you in dealing with a difficult person.

ACKNOWLEDGE THE ENERGY BODY

With some difficult people, the dynamic is so thick you can actually feel it. I call this an "energy body" and it is something palpable that exists between the difficult person and those around them. The energy body can take many forms. It can be a draining energy, controlling energy, toxic energy, or sad energy. Whatever form it takes, the energy body can affect not only the people who have to deal directly with the difficult person, but also those around them. If you remarry into a family with a difficult person who causes disruption, and you're exposed to their dysfunctional relationships long enough, it becomes a visceral experience for you too. You and your partner may see that sometimes it can take several days after being around that person or situation to feel normal again.

If you remarry into a family with a difficult person who causes disruption, and you're exposed to their dysfunctional relationships long enough, it becomes a visceral experience for you too.

For example, let's say you and your new husband are invited to a birthday party at the home of his sister, who has always been a disrupter in his family. That morning, you notice your spouse seems grumpy and irritated, snapping at you for no reason. As the day goes on, the tension rises, and your normally good-natured spouse turns downright sullen. On the drive there, he grips the steering wheel and says nothing. At the birthday party, he puts on a smile, makes small talk, and is polite to everyone. Likewise, his sister acts gracious the whole time. Even though everybody is on their best behavior, you can feel the energy body between them.

After the party, your husband sinks back into his bad mood, and you can still feel the energy body surrounding him. The next day, almost as if he has a hangover, it takes him until lunchtime to shed the energy body and go back to normal. That's the power of the energy body.

In some blended families, you may be dealing with a loaded dynamic that has been playing out for a long time, perhaps for years before you came along. The family may realize that the person's behavior is dysfunctional, and they may have developed workarounds to manage that person. You may have initiated some open communication with your new partner about the problem person, and you may both be learning to put tools in place and to work together to address it on a deeper level.

In the meantime, you may still be feeling the energy body whenever family events come up and you have to face the difficult person. Your partner may try to pull you into the drama as a way to normalize it or to let off steam. Or they may involve others in the drama simply as part of a long-standing pattern. After you have left the difficult person or situation, you may both experience a sort of energy body hangover for a good twenty-four hours. Because there is a residue of energy that may linger, there can be a backlash of emotions. You may have to deal with your partner as they try to de-stress from the effects of the dysfunctional dynamic that just played out.

If you're faced with this kind of situation where your new partner is dealing with an enmeshed or dysfunctional relationship with a difficult relative, take measures to protect yourself. It's important to keep it from damaging you too. Take advantage of the following strategies to help you handle the situation and cope with the energy body.

Set boundaries.

You don't have to put yourself in the line of fire if it isn't your relationship to sort out. Limit how much you allow yourself to be involved with the difficult person and in the dysfunctional dynamic. Keeping a healthy distance can help you avoid getting dragged down by the energy body.

Give your partner some space and offer calm loving support if you can.

When your partner has to deal with the disrupter, they may need some alone time after an encounter. Offer them some space in a calm way. Take a walk, have a cup of tea, or read a book. Just remove your energy from the mix and give your partner some alone time to de-stress from their feelings. Let them approach you when they're ready. Your calm action will help send a message to your partner that their dealings with the disrupter impact you and your relationship too. When your partner begins to understand that the attitude they bring home after interacting with this disrupter can be toxic and that you will stay out of the line of fire, they may make the effort not to take their emotions out on you.

Drop it. Don't allow the difficult person to dominate your life together even when they are not there. Don't make that person the focus of your relationship.

Schedule time to talk about the situation.

If either of you needs to discuss the matter do it at a time when tensions aren't high. If necessary, consider seeking the help of a counselor.

HOW TO REACT IN THE HEAT OF THE MOMENT

Long-term strategies can help you and other family members forge a path to better relationships with a difficult person, but how should you respond in the heat of the moment when that person is displaying out-of-control behavior? You may be tempted to lash back at them with anger. You may feel like crying. You may want to turn your back on them and storm out of the room. Before retaliating in any way, take a step back and keep their limitations in mind. Here are some tips to help you survive an emotional emergency.

- Breathe and count to ten before you respond to someone who is pushing your buttons.

- Try to respond from a position of love.

- Set an example of good behavior.

- Try your best to listen and respond with honest answers.

- Don't take it personally. Remember that this person was likely out of control long before you came along.

- Let the person know you're uncomfortable with the situation and suggest you connect at a later time.

LONG-TERM STRATEGIES TO IMPROVE RELATIONSHIPS WITH DIFFICULT PEOPLE

After years of working with blended families, I have come up with a number of tips to help you deal with difficult people. These strategies are intended to alleviate your frustration, preserve your sanity, and help you develop a plan to change long-standing, harmful dynamics.

Get ready for a challenge.
Understand that changing deeply ingrained patterns of behavior takes time and may be met with pushback.

Acknowledge the problem.

The first step to solving any problem is acknowledging its existence. Be honest about the dysfunction that surrounds the difficult person, even if that person is someone you love.

Don't go it alone.

Forget the idea that you can "fix" the difficult person on your own. You'll need the support of other family members who are entangled in the dysfunctional dynamics to work with you. When several people are willing to work together, you can build bridges that lead to healthier relationships.

Distance can be healthy.

Giving yourself some space from the difficult person is a good way to limit your exposure to the conflict. For example, seeing a family member once a month rather than once a week can limit the conflict so the issue becomes more manageable. At family events, you may want to drive separately so your new spouse can stay as long as they wish, and you can leave early if you feel it is necessary.

Know the players in the drama.

Go beyond the surface to determine what each person in the dysfunctional relationship is seeking. For example, the difficult person may be seeking signs of support or loyalty while others in the relationship may be seeking greater independence or gratitude. Each person's particular needs should be taken into consideration before compromises can be created. Be aware too that several survival instincts may kick in. Some people may want to run away from the problem, while others may have the instinct to fight. Recognize their typical reactions.

Patience is required.

Relational roadblocks and emotional conflicts are complicated and can be exhausting. Rather than leading with your emotions, consider taking a break in order to allow the heart and the mind to come together.

Cutting someone off is not always the solution.

Your first instinct may be to end the relationship, but unless someone is consistently toxic, poses a danger to family members, or is unwilling or unable to work things out with others, don't cut them off from the family. Walking away from the difficult person won't fix the problem and will leave the other family members in the dysfunctional dynamic. Just keep strong boundaries around them and limit the control they have on events, family members, and decision-making. In addition, let them know they are not being pushed out, only regulated.

Practice the art of compromise.

Dig deep within yourself to find ways to continue engaging with those who are dysfunctional in a way that doesn't punish other family members. Agree to show up in a loving way for special occasions.

Understand that dysfunction is not isolated or static.

Problems do not remain the same and are not only one single thing. They change as we change. Often as we resolve certain issues, other issues come up. The problems a person has in their twenties, for example, are different from the problems they face in their fifties. Be aware that issues surface at different times with different people.

Develop compassion.

At some point, you may have a bad day and you may lash out uncharacteristically at other family members. If this happens, you would want your family to show you compassion rather than cutting you off or turning against you. Likewise, learn to develop compassion not only for the person who is displaying bad behavior, but also for the other family members who are experiencing their own particular pain and personal limitations.

Decide if it's a deal breaker for you.

Before you enter into a long-term commitment with someone who is allowing a damaged person to lead their family, consider if you can live with unacceptable behavior that may not change. If you can't change it and you can't live with it, you may need to move on.

Seek outside help.

Finding a family therapist or counselor to work with at this point is often a great help. They will be an important part of the support team for you and your family as you deal with an out-of-control family member.

DIFFICULT PEOPLE DOs & DON'Ts

- Do acknowledge the problems a difficult person creates for the blended family.

- Do look beyond a difficult person's bad behavior to seek what's behind their actions.

- Do recognize issues with anger and control.

- Do accept that people may be damaged, fragile, or suffering from mental health issues.

- Do be aware of the energy body that exists between people in dysfunctional relationships.

- Do be compassionate.

- Do learn how to react in the heat of the moment.

- Don't let the most damaged person in the family take the lead.

- Don't let anger become your family's default mode for communication.

- Don't let a cycle of anger be passed down from one generation to the next.

- Don't expect more from family members than they can offer.

- Don't just cut people off. Make this the last resort.

NEXT STEPS

- Consider what might be behind a difficult person's behavior.

- Examine the limitations each person has in the situation.

- Take notice of how the energy body is affecting you and others around you.

- Be aware of how to react to emotional emergencies.

- Ask yourself if the dysfunctional dynamic with the difficult person is beyond repair and if it is a deal breaker for you.

CHAPTER HIGHLIGHTS

- In many blended families, we let the most dysfunctional one make all the decisions.

- Difficult people tend to have issues with anger and a need to control others.

- Changing long-standing dysfunctional behavior is not a quick fix.

- Accept that all the people involved in a dysfunctional dynamic have limitations.

- With difficult people, the dynamic can be so thick you can feel it. This is called an energy body.

- Develop long-term strategies to deal with difficult people and have a set of tools you can use in emotional emergencies.

CHAPTER EIGHT

THE SEVEN MOST HARMFUL SOCIAL TABOOS FOR BLENDED FAMILIES

"In search of my mother's garden, I found my own."
— *Alice Walker*

Have you ever felt uncomfortable about putting up pictures that include your former family members? Have you ever cringed because you accidently called your new partner by your former spouse's name? Do you ever feel self-conscious while telling your new partner a story that involves your past relationship?

On the other hand, have you ever felt slighted because your stepchildren said they missed their real mom/dad in front of you? Have you ever felt a little stab in your heart because your biological children told you how great your former partner's new spouse is? Have you ever felt hurt or rejected because an extended family member chose not to attend an event because you were going to be there?

You're not alone. Many people are bothered or triggered by these things. These negative feelings stem mainly from long-standing social taboos regarding divorce, remarriage, and blended families. Why do we perpetuate these myths? In this chapter I've identified the seven most harmful social taboos and how you can keep them from tripping up your tribe.

Social Taboo #1: You should never acknowledge your former partner or former life around your new partner.

It's time to shake up the myth that people in blended families need to tiptoe around past lives. Why do we interpret acknowledging our past as a threat to our current relationship? Is it because we feel grief and don't want to relive the past in a painful way? Are we jealous or threatened by people from our new partner's past? Is it because we feel this indicates that the person we are in love with is still in love with their former partner? Is it because we feel we are being compared to their former partner and perhaps don't match up? Could it be because this is a reminder that our partner was in love with someone other than us in the past? What kind of atmosphere does this create for us if we feel we are not allowed to talk about certain things in front of our partner even though we would easily share them with our best friends?

We know that some of these questions will be a part of life once we have had more than one partner in our lives. We know that once we have children with someone and share a family, we are no longer virgins with clean slates. Remember the gifts in this; remember that you and your partner have grown from all your experiences and that the two of you would not be who you have become without all your previous life experiences. It seems unfair that we can be hurt so easily by our partner's past when we have a past too. We shouldn't have to hide it or pretend it didn't happen.

Truly accepting someone means accepting their past and, in fact, celebrating it as a part of who they are. If you can acknowledge that all your past relationship experiences are what brought you both to the place you are today, then you may be able to find some gratitude for those who were part of your new partner's past.

Truly accepting someone means accepting their past and, in fact, celebrating it as a part of who they are.

If you're authentically interested in understanding the family dynamics surrounding your new partner, it helps to know their history. This is why it is so important to maintain open communication about former partners. Embracing the truth that your partner has a past will allow valuable pieces of their life story to be brought to light instead of hidden. When you invest in each other's relationships—not just the one you share together—it helps tie all aspects of the former life with the present life. Your pasts become intertwined instead of forbidden "BM" ("before me") territory.

When you and your new partner both feel you have the freedom to share and remember past events, memories, losses, and life lessons, it will allow greater intimacy and trust to develop.

This applies to extended family members too. Show them respect for their pasts and make space for them to feel safe in sharing their lives with you.

TODD AND JESSICA: LIVING WITHOUT A PAST

Jessica was at a dinner party with her new husband, Todd, and some of his friends when he started telling a story about raising his children with his first wife. When Todd got to one part of the story when his former wife said something really funny, everybody at the table laughed. Everybody except Jessica, that is. She found herself catching her breath. A stream of thoughts raced through her mind. "Oh, he's talking about another woman." "He raised children with someone else." "Was his first wife funnier than I am?" "Do his friends wish he was still with her?"

Later that night, Jessica had to take a step back and think about why she had reacted so strongly to the mere mention of Todd's first wife. Of course, she knew Todd had been married previously. They had spent nearly twenty years together. And she realized that the mother of his grown children would always be in their lives to some extent. Jessica decided it was up to her to stop taking it so personally when Todd mentioned his first wife.

The truth was Todd and Jessica had four grown children between the two of them. In addition to raising those children with other partners, they had attended weddings, purchased homes, and taken vacations with those individuals. She couldn't expect him to simply erase all those memories; the same way she couldn't pretend those experiences hadn't happened in her life.

She decided she wanted the children, as well as their extended family and friends, to feel safe and secure in sharing memories about their lives prior to her marriage to Todd, so she began working to evolve her thought processes. She routinely reminds herself that everything she and Todd have been through is part of what brought them to the place they are now. She began to view the man she fell in love with as a culmination of all the love and experiences he had been through. She realized she should be thankful for all the people who came before her because they were part of shaping him into the person he is now.

Jessica understood that she wouldn't be the partner she was now if she hadn't experienced so much with her first husband. She made a conscious choice that in order to create a deeper, happier, and more intimate relationship, she needed to make it okay to share and talk with each other or in front of each other about their pasts. Jessica started encouraging the adult children to share stories about their lives growing up with their other parents and to talk about their relationships and celebrations with other members of the growing blended family. Jessica found that celebrating—rather than erasing—their past lives led to greater intimacy and strengthened the family bonds.

Social Taboo #2: Former partners should never attend the same event.

So many of my clients have told me they won't attend a school event or birthday party for their children if their former partner will be there. When I ask them why, they often look at me blankly and have no response other than, "Well, because it might be uncomfortable." I usually follow up by asking, "Uncomfortable for whom?" Some admit they are the one who will feel uncomfortable.

For many of them, this is the very first time they have actively thought about this. They realize they had simply accepted the notion that former partners shouldn't attend events together. It's very rewarding for me to see them go through the thought process and come to the realization that this is, in fact, a myth.

Although the increased contact may lead to some conflict initially, it will ultimately increase healing as you commit yourself to what is best for everyone versus what is best for yourself.

Children want and need both their parents, and the more time they can spend with both of you the better. The children love both of you regardless of whatever injustices might have occurred between the two of you. The time you spend with your children is not about you; it's about their needs. Stop thinking about how you feel and start thinking about how they feel.

Adopt the attitude that if anyone in the room should be forced to be uncomfortable, it should be you, not your children. Take opportunities to be involved in your children's events even if your former spouse will also be in attendance. Try not to spend the entire time thinking about how uncomfortable you are. Instead, keep your focus on being there for your children.

Although the increased contact may lead to some conflict initially, it will ultimately increase healing as you commit yourself to what is best for everyone versus what is best for yourself.

Social Taboo #3: Former partners should divide up friends and family members.

After separating their assets in a divorce, many former couples try to divide up their friends and family members as if they were possessions. In general, nobody blinks an eye when this happens. Forcing friends and family members to choose sides, however, punishes everyone. You and your former partner may each lose connections to people you loved. Even more devastating, however, is that your children can lose family, community, and support systems. The practice of dividing and separating friends and family creates more dysfunction.

In some cases, forcing friends and family to choose sides comes from a need to micromanage situations for your own benefit rather than the benefit of the entire blended family.

This separation or compartmentalization is a way of coping that promotes self-protection rather than self-awareness. The question is, do you want short-term self-protection more than you want long-term healing?

No one has to divorce a community, and no one should ever ask you to divorce your friends or family members. Likewise, you should never ask friends or family to divorce your former partner. Working together and being respectful of each other provides a support system that will benefit everyone in the extended blended family.

DENISE AND MARGARET: THE ULTIMATUM

Denise was married to Marlon for ten years and had a seven-year-old daughter named Shanay. From the day Shanay was born, Denise's mother, Margaret, was a constant in their lives. A doting grandmother, she offered a lot of support by taking care of Shanay whenever the couple needed help. She also often drove the little girl to after-school activities and to appointments. Margaret had also forged a close bond with her son-in-law, and they spoke regularly.

Shortly after their tenth anniversary, Marlon asked Denise for a divorce. She was shocked and tried to save the marriage, but Marlon was ready to move on. Denise was so angry with him that she gave Margaret an ultimatum: "It's me or Marlon." Denise told Margaret that she could no longer invite Marlon into her house or communicate with him in any way. And if Margaret didn't comply with her wishes, she would cut off contact with her completely. Margaret would lose her daughter and her granddaughter from her life. Devastated, Margaret made the only choice she could, and she lost her relationship with her son-in-law. Denise's emotional blackmail to separate her mother from her former partner did inflict pain on him, but unfortunately he wasn't the only one who got hurt. Margaret and Shanay both suffered too.

Social Taboo #4: Stepparents and stepchildren can never love each other the way they love their biological relatives.

One of my clients told me that when she remarried a man who had two children, a friend told her, "You'll never love his kids the way you love your own." As a society, this kind of careless thinking sets up roadblocks for stepparents and stepchildren. Yes, there will likely be awkwardness, missteps, and challenges as you and your stepchildren develop a relationship, but the bond you create can deepen into a permanent love like you have with your biological children. This may not happen for everyone, but knowing it is possible can make you more open to allowing it to happen.

Social Taboo #5: If one partner is hurting, it's okay to punish the former partner so they hurt too.

In our society, it's very common for one partner in a divorcing couple to want to punish the other partner and to want everyone else to punish them too. This is seen as normal and acceptable. When one person tries to unleash destruction, war, and social excommunication on their former partner, nobody questions them. This punishment can continue after remarriage and into your life with a new blended family. This old idea that requires everyone to suffer needs to evolve.

You don't have to follow this unhealthy tradition. One way to create a better path is to accept that your partner hurt you and stop punishing them for it. Engage in kind communication with your former partner. This increases the opportunities for personal healing and minimizes the damage that seeps into other family or romantic relationships. How does staying in kind communication help us heal? This practice creates a more peaceful environment as opposed to a war zone. As you've seen in this book, creating a war zone impacts the entire family in a negative way. On the other hand, creating a peaceful environment helps everybody heal and move forward in their lives. Acceptance is a vital component for creating peaceful relationships.

Make a decision about your own behavior. Decide that the acceptance and kindness you extend to someone who may not deserve it is a practice of peace. By practicing acceptance and peace, you can create something different, something new, something better—not just for yourself, but for future generations.

LINDA AND CLIFF: SEPARATION AND PUNISHMENT

Linda and Cliff, who married and had two children, lived outside Seattle where Linda had grown up. She loved being able to see her family and longtime friends on a regular basis. When Cliff was offered a major promotion for a position in his company, he and Linda decided together that they couldn't pass it up even though it was halfway across the country. She agreed to relocate and left behind the life she loved. Years later, Cliff told Linda he wanted a divorce and walked out on her.

Devastated and hurt, Linda decided she was going to take the children and move back to the Seattle area. Considering he was still supporting the family financially, Cliff couldn't give up his job so he was unable to make the move with them. Although Linda had initially agreed to move with Cliff, she felt justified in going back home because he had left her and therefore broken the commitment they had made together. After initially getting joint custody, Linda took Cliff back to court to fight him to gain sole custody of their two children. The judge's ruling left Cliff brokenhearted. He could barely stand to say goodbye to them at the airport when they left.

Linda relished the sight of Cliff in pain. He had caused her so much anguish that she wanted him to suffer too. But in her decision to punish Cliff she didn't take into consideration that she was also hurting her two children. She was acting out of her own selfish desire to relocate rather than thinking about what their children wanted or what would be best for them. Although it was true that Cliff had treated Linda badly, he had been a loving and involved parent. Even after the separation, he saw the children almost daily, drove them to and from school events and appointments, helped them with their homework, and spent time cycling with them. The children loved him and wanted him in their lives on a daily basis.

By moving the children out of state, Linda had not only separated the children from their father, but she had also lost a helpful parenting partner. Now Linda was overstressed with the burden of raising them alone. The children picked up on her negative energy and struggled to make friends at their new school. They missed their father and had to do a lot of things for themselves that he used to do for them.

Although it's understandable that Linda may have wanted to punish Cliff because he had hurt her, her actions resulted in negative consequences for their children. With her punishing behavior, she won the battle to hurt her former partner. In the long run, however, she had created more damage and stress for all of them.

Social Taboo #6: When you're a stepparent, it's best to stay out of any problems involving the stepchildren.

One of my clients told me, "The problems my wife's kids are having aren't my problem. She needs to handle it." Another client, who married a man with three boys from a previous marriage, complained to me about how badly the boys behaved. "They aren't my kids, so what do I care?" The myth that a stepparent isn't supposed to be involved in the parenting of their stepchildren needs to change.

If you're a stepparent, you need to be involved in the raising of the stepchildren. As you saw in chapter 6, you may not want to take a strong disciplinarian stance from the start, but you do need to address any issues with your partner and present a unified front. By working together as a team to find solutions for dysfunctional behavior, you will be strengthening the entire blended family unit.

By working together as a team to find solutions for dysfunctional behavior, you will be strengthening the entire blended family unit.

Social Taboo #7: If you distance your first family, it will make it easier to create a healthy second family.

As you've seen in this book, some people cling to the myth that if they can start over with a clean slate then their second family will be perfect. This is one of the most harmful myths surrounding remarriage and second families. Distancing yourself from your first family as a way to create a nuclear second family is devastating to first-family children. In most cases, the pain and hurt the first-family children experience as a result of such treatment will eventually impact the second family as well.

I urge all my clients to discard this myth categorically. Your first family will not go away. Make the effort to heal the wounds and to address any dysfunctional behaviors in the first family so you can integrate those children into the second family. Include, don't exclude—this is the best approach for creating a healthy blended family.

SOCIAL TABOO DOs & DON'Ts

- Do encourage your new partner and stepchildren to share their whole lives with you, not just the life they have lived since you arrived in it.

- Do show up for your children even if your former partner will be there and it makes you uncomfortable.

- Do allow friends and family to be a resource for everyone.

- Do stay open-minded about the bond you can develop with your stepchildren.

- Do maintain your focus on what's best for your children even though you may be hurting.

- Do offer support to your new partner in working through issues with stepchildren.

- Do make an effort to heal your first family.

- Don't compartmentalize parts of your life.

- Don't punish your children by not attending events because you don't want to face your former partner.

- Don't force friends or family members to pledge allegiance to you or cut them off from your former partner.

- Don't shut yourself off to your stepchildren.

- Don't hurt others in your quest for revenge against your former partner.

- Don't ignore issues with stepchildren.

- Don't alienate your first family.

NEXT STEPS

- Take note if you feel hurt, anxious, or uncomfortable when your new partner talks about their life before you. Explore what you can do to learn to accept their former life.

- Consider ways to control your emotions so you can attend your children's events with your former partner.

- See if you can view your friends and family as a helpful support network for everyone rather than as possessions you and your former spouse need to claim.

- Open your heart to the possibility of deep love for your stepchildren.

- Ask yourself if you are unnecessarily punishing anyone else in an effort to compensate for your pain.

- Work with your new spouse to find positive ways to address any issues with your stepchildren.

- Think about how you can help heal your first family so it can help strengthen your second family.

CHAPTER HIGHLIGHTS

- Social Taboo #1: You should never acknowledge your former partner or former life around your new partner.

- Social Taboo #2: Former partners should never attend the same event.

- Social Taboo #3: Former partners should divide up friends and family members.

- Social Taboo #4: Stepparents and stepchildren can never love each other the way they love their biological relatives.

- Social Taboo #5: If one partner is hurting, it's okay to punish the former partner so they hurt too.

- Social Taboo #6: When you're a stepparent, it's best to stay out of any problems involving the stepchildren.

- Social Taboo #7: If you distance your first family, it will make it easier to create a healthy second family.

CHAPTER NINE

LESSONS FROM FAMILIES WORKING TOGETHER AND BECOMING HEALTHIER TRIBES

"The noblest pleasure is the joy of understanding."
— *Leonardo da Vinci*

One of the best ways to learn how to make your blended family work is to take cues from other tribes who are doing it right. In addition to helping my clients discover better ways to address issues in their families, I always remind them to celebrate the things they are doing that work. In this chapter you'll meet seven families who have come up with powerful solutions that you may want to implement in your family too.

JEFF AND CARRIE: LEARNING TO FACE ISSUES WITH FAMILY MEETINGS

Jeff and Carrie, who each had children from previous marriages, have discovered that having regular family meetings where anyone can speak out about anything that is bothering them is a great way to deal with issues before they become a major problem.

It also created a way for them to stay in touch with things that are going on in their children's lives with regularity and allows them to give their children some good attention. Jeff and Carrie have found that family meetings also serve to create a sense of respect for each other's feelings and emotions.

One of the things Jeff and Carrie like most about family meetings is that they provide an opportunity for their children to get to know them in a different way. They become vulnerable when they share themselves with the children—talking about how they are feeling about things and giving the children a bit of insight into their daily lives.

Having regular family meetings is something I routinely suggest to my clients. No matter how old your children are, it is great to give and receive the gift of listening without interruption. And the younger your children can learn this skill the better. When you call a family meeting, you can come together in a circle or just sit around a table—whatever works best for your family. You can even use Skype or FaceTime to include family members who don't live in the same house.

No matter how old your children are, it is great to give and receive the gift of listening without interruption.

I like the idea of a talking stick or some other object that is meaningful to you. Whoever has the stick is the one who gets to share while the others listen. When that person has finished talking, they pass the stick to the next person. There is no cross talk until everyone has had a chance to share. Sometimes setting a time limit for talking—fifteen minutes or so—is a good idea. It is a way for everyone to express how they are feeling, but it is not a time for answers or decisions to be made. It is just a safe time to share feelings as a family. If you decide to have a dialogue about what was shared in the circle, you should do that afterward with the agreement of the whole family, if possible.

ELLIOT AND SARAH: KEEPING A SECOND (OR THIRD) WEDDING SIMPLE

Elliot and Sarah were getting married and wanted all their adult children from previous marriages to be included in the ceremony. The idea sounded wonderful, but they began to run into roadblocks—scheduling problems, conflicting thoughts on the ceremony, and so on. It also began stirring up a lot of emotions.

Eventually, they realized that a big traditional wedding was just too complicated. There were so many people to bring together and so many

different traditions and expectations on the different sides of the blending families that they decided to forego the big wedding. Instead they
got married quietly on their own so they could focus on each other and
not the moods or needs of others. Then they threw a party for the whole
family where they did a ring exchange and a toast to their union. This
gathering was a much more relaxed occasion with music, dancing, and
fun. Everyone felt comfortable, and it minimized the drama.

*By keeping it loving and simple,
they were able to include everyone
without any emotional upheaval.*

One of the powerful things about this couple's decision is that they
were not overwhelmed by their children's needs or emotions regarding
the wedding. Sarah was grateful that she had been able to focus on her
vows and her new partner during the ceremony. Because of that she
was able to enjoy the party without worrying about how everyone else
was feeling. The idea that it was just a party, not a wedding, changed
everything. They were already married, and this fact lifted the emotional
weight off everyone's shoulders. By keeping it loving and simple, they
were able to include everyone without any emotional upheaval.

KEN AND JAMIE: CO-PARENTING WITH LOVE

When Ken and Jamie married, they each came with two grown
children. They fought about the children and their different parenting
styles. Oftentimes one of the children would wind up their parent and it

would create distance and discord between Ken and Jamie. We all know it is a social taboo to talk negatively about your partner's children, their parents, or even their pets. But, when you are a blended family you have to get past that. If you don't, the children may use it as a way to wedge distance between you and your new partner. And these patterns can be very hard to break.

With counseling, they adopted a new tactic. They became a united front.

After enough fights regarding the demands and difficulties with their children, Jamie requested that she and Ken see a counselor to hash out some boundaries. The most important thing they discovered was that when they let the children come between them, it made them vulnerable, and that's when their fights would start.

With counseling, they adopted a new tactic. They became a united front. Any requests or concerns from their adult children now had to go through both Ken and Jamie. And the two of them always discussed their response first before making any promises to the children. In essence, they started putting their own well-being first in regards to their grown children. The more they did so, the more the children began to accept it from them, and they started treating their stepparent with more respect. Because their own parent was treating their partner with respect and standing with them as a united front, it created a strong alliance and the group became a family.

Ken and Jamie's situation involved grown children, who were already living on their own and capable of taking care of themselves. In this type of scenario, you can often deal with the issues by working together with your new partner and a counselor. Each parent can impart the new strategies you have come up with to their own children. If you are going through issues with younger children who are living with you, I strongly suggest family counseling as a means of learning how to co-parent and work through issues together.

MARCUS AND RICK: TEAMING UP

When Marcus married Rick's former wife, he became a stepparent to their two young sons. Rick understood that his two sons would be spending a large amount of time with Marcus, and it was very important for him to get to know this man who would be influencing his sons. Rick was really hoping they could forge a friendship of sorts or at least a good co-parenting relationship. He felt relieved to find out that Marcus felt the same and was willing to get to know Rick and work out a friendship.

It was a different kind of "boys' night out", but it worked for them.

In the beginning there were some rough spots. They were in new territory, and they stumbled and struggled to agree on how some things should be handled with the boys. But the two men came to a decision to set aside their issues and began taking the two boys to different events together, fun things they could all enjoy—two dads, two sons. It was a different kind of "boys' night out", but it worked for them. It created a way for the two men to grow to understand each other better, and it bonded them in their primary goal, which was to raise two healthy, wonderful boys.

After some time, Marcus and Kristen—Rick's former wife and the mother of his boys—had a baby of their own, another boy. To this day Rick is known as Uncle Rick to their bio child and is included in that boy's life too. Now they have an extended tribe, and the two dads make sure that all the children in their blended family feel loved by each of them.

TAYLOR, BRITT, CARSON, AND DASHIELL: A SIBLING SUCCESS STORY

When their mom married a new man, teens Taylor and Britt became older siblings to elementary school kids Carson and Dashiell. Their parents knew that the different age groups of their children would bring with them different needs, and it could have caused friction. They made every effort to do things for both age groups that were appropriate—movie nights with the older ones, camping trips geared toward the older children's needs, and then simpler backyard camping for the younger ones. They regulated bedtimes to suit the needs of both age groups.

> *The older children embraced their roles as mentors to the younger ones.*

It was a bit more stressful for the parents because they were juggling the very different needs of children with an age gap, but it was the glue that made all the children feel at home. Because they all felt loved, they began to be able to share their home and their parents with a happy attitude. Actually, the older children embraced their roles as mentors to the younger ones. They decided that once a week they would do something fun with them without the parents around, and this helped them bond as siblings.

CECILIA AND MARIAH: FAMILY GET-TOGETHERS

Cecilia is married to Ben, whose forty-three year old daughter is Mariah. Cecilia and Mariah have always been the holiday and family event organizers for their respective families. This could have led to the two of them butting heads or trying to control holiday planning, but once they became part of a blended family, they decided to work together to trade off planning.

> *They decided to work together to trade off planning.*

Cecilia plans and hosts Thanksgiving, and Mariah handles the winter holiday. Together, they share organizing duties for a summer bash and other birthday dinners. They support each other and remind each other how nice it is to have a break from being the only one doing the gatherings. And they each take pleasure now in relaxing and enjoying the holiday party where they get to be a guest rather than the hostess. As a matter of fact, they have each discovered that they love to be a guest.

TAD AND MICHIKO: KEEPING ADULT CHILDREN IN THE LOOP

Tad has two adult children and Michiko has three from previous marriages. Michiko communicates with her three adult children and their spouses to keep them up to date on family matters as well as making plans for gatherings and celebrations and such. When they first married, Tad expected Michiko to handle the communications with his offspring as well because his former wife had always taken on that duty. But he realized he couldn't expect his new partner to step into that role, so he took it on himself.

To his surprise, he grew to love this new role.

It was a big change for Tad. He was used to being a bystander and having someone else keep him informed of events and plans. Now he was being asked to make decisions and communicate back and forth with his family in a new way. Uncomfortable in this position at first, he found that his relationships with his children grew and became stronger. He evolved into an important family communicator. Sometimes he even came up with ideas about what they should do as a family, made plans, called for reservations, and even bought gifts. It was a new role for Tad that he never would have taken on if he hadn't become part of a blended family. To his surprise, he grew to love this new role.

I love telling my clients about Tad. In my mind, he represents the unexpected joy of being part of a blended family. By opening himself up to a new role, he experienced personal growth and found deeper love with his children. Like I tell my clients, when you're blending families, open your heart and open your mind. You never know what new joy you may discover.

HEALTHY TRIBE DOs & DON'Ts

- Do listen to family members without interrupting them.

- Do try to minimize emotional issues surrounding a new wedding.

- Do talk to your partner before making promises to the children.

- Do let children know they are loved by all the parents.

- Do encourage older siblings to spend time with younger ones.

- Do include other family members in holiday planning.

- Do open your mind and heart to taking on a new role in the family.

———————— o ————————

- Don't close yourself off to new ways to communicate with your family.

- Don't cater to other family members' emotional needs instead of your own.

- Don't let children drive a wedge between you and your new partner.

- Don't shut out former partners.

- Don't ignore older children by focusing on younger children's needs.

- Don't be too controlling when it comes to holiday planning.

- Don't expect your spouse to handle communications with your children.

NEXT STEPS

- Consider scheduling a family meeting and see how it goes.

- Allow yourself to think of your own needs when planning your wedding.

- Try counseling with your new partner if you have parenting issues.

- Open your heart to the possibility of a friendship with your spouse's former partner.

- Ask yourself if you are being fair to all the children in the new blended family.

- Work with your new family members to create low-stress family get-togethers.

- Think about how you can help keep your children updated on family matters.

CHAPTER HIGHLIGHTS

- Holding family meetings on a regular basis can be a powerful way to unite the family.

- Keeping a second or third wedding simple may minimize emotional issues.

- Becoming a united front with your new partner can strengthen your bond.

- Try to think of your new partner's former partner as a teammate.

- Find ways to help siblings of different ages coexist.

- Work with other family members to take the stress out of holiday planning.

- Agree to take on the role of keeping your own children in the loop.

ACKNOWLEDGEMENTS

I am especially grateful to Robert Baruc, my husband, my number-one supporter, and my business partner. Without your steadfast love, support, and encouragement, this book would not be here. I love you, and I thank you from the bottom of my heart.

Thank you to my beautiful blended family for inspiring me. Thank you for working together as a group, trying new things, listening to your heart, and being inclusive and loving. I know it's not always easy, so I want to recognize you for being there for me and allowing me to share a part of my life through our stories. You reaffirm my faith in humanity and in our ability to love each other.

I want to express my gratitude to my editor, Frances Sharpe. You worked with such grace that the process was seamless. I am eternally grateful to you.

I give my heartfelt gratitude to Aaron Davis for making this book into something beautiful to hold in my hands as well as to read.

I'm grateful to Rebecca Baruc for bringing her artistic vision by creating this beautiful hand painted cover artwork.

Thank you Denise Acosta, my assistant, for your support, knowledge and for bringing an air of joy to the project.

Thank you to Melanie Ariken Ward for your thoroughness and uplifting spirit.

Thank you Ni'coel Stark for your contribution to this project.

ABOUT WENDY SMITH BARUC

Wendy Smith Baruc is a marriage counselor and relationship coach. She is married to Robert Baruc and between the two of them, they have five grown children and two grandchildren. She has been a practitioner in the healing arts for over thirty years. She has found that her greatest insights, growth, and knowledge have come from her own life experiences as well as the intimate work she does with her clients.

Couples counseling has reinforced her faith in human nature and committed relationships. Wendy considers it an honor to be part of the greatest adventure a person can take on—facing one's self through the commitment to another. She is inspired by watching couples transform in front of her eyes, with their openness and willingness to participate in this process.

Wendy coaches, supports, and guides couples, families, and blended families. She navigates and mediates as they work through difficult issues, helping them create new behaviors to support the longevity of their relationship. Wendy works to help couples and families improve their communication, interpreting what she hears and sees happening between them. She has found that with strategic input one discovers the underlying dynamics of their conflicts. Once given these tools, couples are capable of getting through the challenges they face.

For more information about Wendy, visit: **wendysmithbaruc.com**